Exposing Socialism for What It Truly Is

A System That Has Always Left Ruins in Its Paths

Moses Oluwole, Ph.D.

Dedication

I, Moses Oluwole, would like to dedicate this book to my Lord Jesus Christ, my loving darling Dr. Oladoyin Oluwole, family, friends, peers, and others who have helped me in my life journey and given me the confidence and inspiration to express myself and my ideologies. Without them, I would never be in this position nor would I have reached my true potential.

Acknowledgment

I like to thank my precious darling, Dr. Oladoyin Oluwole, and every person who made this journey possible for me and allowed me to communicate the true horrors of socialism and communism. It is my hope that through this book, the people of the USA, particularly the youth, will understand these two flawed and manipulative political systems and never enable these systems to take root in our beloved country.

About the Author

Hailing from Nigeria, I, Moses Oluwole, didn't have great aspirations in my early youth. I took life at face value and didn't have the opportunity to evaluate my life and think of greener pastures. However, despite my humble beginnings, through the Grace of God, I managed to attain a Ph.D. in Industrial Chemistry from Germany and have been a Chemistry teacher for most of my life. I was able to attend the most competitive schools in my home country and abroad and I couldn't be more thankful to the Almighty for giving me this opportunity. Now, I wish to communicate my experiences to the nation's youth and enlighten them regarding the real challenges of the USA and how, as a nation, we can overcome them.

Preface

This book will shed light on the history of socialism and communism and how these sociopolitical systems crippled the nations that adhered to them. In later chapters, we will learn the true face of socialism and why its influence must be curbed in the USA as soon as possible. Moreover, we will also discuss the negative role of so-called *modernist* or *liberal* teachers of the present day and how they are misguiding the nation's youth at a rapid pace that must be eliminated in its infancy.

Contents

Page Left Blank Intentionally

Chapter 1
Introduction

"The Spirit of the Lord God is upon Me,
Because the Lord has anointed Me
To preach good tidings to the poor;
He has sent Me to heal the brokenhearted,
To proclaim liberty to the captives,
And the opening of the prison to those who are bound;"

-Isaiah 61:1

Everyone is born with a purpose in life. We all have our callings, and it is essential to identify and cherish them, even if it is not as great as that of the Bible characters. The lives of many saints motivate us to know that God can use the most ordinary and flawed men and women for His glory.

This inspiration keeps us going even when times get tough. Our lives are predestined for greater things. Even if we do not know what the future holds, we can be sure that God holds the future and that He has abundant blessings in store for us. Therefore, our purpose on earth is solely to be His image-bearers, to lift up the oppressed and depressed, and motivate them. We have to be the source of light to the whole of humanity. My name is Moses Oluwole. I am a married man and a father to four children and four grandchildren. I'm a retired Chemistry professor and researcher and now engaged in writing Christian books.

My life was never extraordinary. I am an average person with my own set of flaws and weaknesses. I was by no means privileged, but by God's grace, I was able to attend the highly competitive Government College, Ibadan, Nigeria. After that, I got my master's degree in chemistry in Britain and my Ph.D. in Industrial Chemistry in Germany. I come from an ordinary background, but God's grace and mercy have brought me thus far. I am deeply humbled by His grace and will forever be grateful for all that He has done and continues to do in my life.

The many narratives in the Bible testify of how God chose the despised and rejected ones, the ones who were weak and ordinary, to be His ambassadors who will proclaim His message of salvation to a lost world. Although they all turned out to be firm believers, none of them came from established backgrounds. In particular, many apostles left everything to follow the Lord Jesus for the rest of their lives. What a privilege! It is indeed a privilege to live a life devoted

2

to Christ. I grew up in a poverty-ridden area of Nigeria. The residents there struggled to feed and protect their families daily. I belonged to the poor class and could, therefore, relate to the challenges of that lifestyle.

As a child, I did everything that a child of my age would do. I had friends with whom I would play all day long. Things were going great, or so I thought until my life was turned upside down when my mother passed away. She had been ill for a long time, and the treatment did not prove to be very effective. She grew weaker and weaker every day and eventually lost her battle to the sickness. Thus, as a 4-year-old child, I was left on my own to bear the weight of her loss.

After her death, my grandmother took over the responsibility of raising me and brought me under her care. Life was never going to be the same again now that I knew my mother was not going to be there for me anymore. But my grandmother's intervention did make things relatively easier. There is no doubt about the love and affection that I received from her, but nothing comes close to a mother's love. It is something that I still miss today, especially when I see how my grandchildren are brought up.

Despite the fact that I had such a rough childhood, I was not religious. Since I was very young when my mother died, my focus in my teenage years was to help my grandmother and provide for her in her old age. But God had a different plan for me. I did not expect my call to come at all if I have to be honest. Nevertheless, it did come at a time when I was a teenager. On December 31, 1956, which was the New Year's Eve, I was on the street in front of our house with other neighborhood kids, when I suddenly had a strange feeling, the like of which I had never had before in my life.

I felt a strange presence that was divine. So, I immediately withdrew from the other kids to a solitary place and closed my eyes and focused solely on that strange Presence. Little did I know that that encounter was going to alter the course of my entire life forever.

I suddenly began to feel the compulsion to go in search of a Church to pray! I instantly obeyed and went on a life-changing adventure to find the Church that was nearest to my house. I searched for over an hour. Eventually, I found this little Catholic Church about two to three miles away from my house. It was a small Catholic chapel and unlit. Since it was pitch dark, I could not see what the place looked like exactly. However, I recall that the building was small, and it was adequate for only about 30 people to fit in comfortably. Using my hands and the rays of the moonlight shining through the glass windows, I made my way to the altar. There, I fell down to prostrate and began to sob for over an hour. Then suddenly, heaven opened, and I began to see different kinds of visions. I left that Church that night a totally changed person. I became very reserved and prayerful, sometimes praying up to 7 hours nonstop.

I hated my past life and began to spend a lot of time alone with God in prayers and the study of the Bible. I began to preach to my former friends to repent and change their ways. It is hard to describe that sudden nocturnal, strange experience. All I can say is that it was a divine visitation by the Holy Spirit. I did not do anything to deserve it since I was just another ordinary boy. Many of my former playmates withdrew from me because they considered me weird.

I believe some other people may have similar experiences since God loves all His children. This was God's way of calling my attention so that He could speak to me. What happened with me was also God's way of showing me that

He had chosen me, and I knew that He wanted me to testify about this glorious encounter. God can use anyone, however learned, illiterate, rich or poor, male or female, young or old. If you look at the people that God chose in the Bible, you will find all of them to be ordinary men and women, judging by worldly standards. 1Corinthians 1:27 states: "But God has chosen the foolish things of the world to put to shame the wise, and God has chosen the weak things of the world to put to shame the mighty things." In God's hands, ordinary people become extraordinary people.

Since I had always wanted to study science, I enrolled to study Chemistry. With the benefit of hindsight, I now believe I ought to have studied Theology, which would have better equipped me for ministry. This wrong choice of science turned out to be a spiritual demotion. My advice to anyone God calls is to obey Him without delay. To God, delayed obedience is the same as disobedience.

I had to pray and fast several times over a period of three years, petitioning God to give me a second chance. Graciously, He did, and therefore I'm fully devoting the rest of my life to His service. My wife and I are currently involved in Church Planting, and we want to help others experience a loving relationship with our blessed Lord and Savior, Jesus Christ. It's indeed a privilege to spread the Word of God all around the world, especially in areas where it has not yet been heard. Indeed, God still has many things to say to the world, and He needs people whom He can use to proclaim His Good news.

Jeremiah 33:3 states:
"Call to Me, and I will answer you,
and show you great and mighty things, which you do not know."

I strongly believe that we are all brothers and sisters in this world, with no one superior to the other on the basis of their racial, ethnic, social, or religious background. God created us after His own image, establishing equality and instructing us to, "Love others just as you want them to love you." Therefore, this statement is the foundation of our God-given task for us for dealing with our neighbors, and it must be fulfilled on a personal level as well as on a global scale. Thus, with the rise of one of the most controversial economic systems in the world today, namely socialism, there is a dire need to revive the true meaning of unity and recreate the balance that has been lost over time.

What is Socialism?

In today's age, countries all over the world have adopted various kinds of lifestyles that are defined by the pace at which they are developing. This development is highly dependent on its economic system, which includes its trade, business, and GDP, as well as the stability within it. In pursuit of this, many countries have embraced socialism as their economic system, and this has, directly and indirectly, impacted other aspects of the life of the citizens.

Socialism is an economic system where everyone in society has equal ownership and rights over the income received from the production of goods and services. In this form of economic system, the government elected by the community members decides the ownership. The government makes legal production and distribution decisions, and individuals rely on the state for everything from food, lifestyles, infrastructure to health care. The governing body also regulates the output and prices of these goods and services.

Socialism has four factors of production, which are entrepreneurship, natural resources, labor, and capital goods. These factors are valued only for their utility to the people.

Socialists take into account individual needs like elders and children; and more significant social needs like health care, security, transportation, education, and natural resources' protection. Everyone in this kind of society receives a share of the income that is based on how much each one has contributed. This system motivates the members to work longer hours if they want to earn more. Workers receive their share after a percentage is subtracted for the common good to keep it fair for everyone.

The Origin of Socialism

In 1841, a Welshman named Robert Owen became the first advocate of socialism. He brought forward various reforms in society and was especially known for establishing the Co-operative Movement. Owen always stood by his belief that all workers should be owners of the companies that they work in and share the profits among themselves. This theory later gained more recognition as Friedrich Engels, and Karl Marx presented their beliefs in support of it. Karl and Friedrich wrote, "The Communist Manifesto," in which they briefly described the meaning of socialism, communism, and capitalism. Out of the many types and definitions of what the terms meant, all led to emphasize that workers must entirely gain the reward of the production. Today, many countries have twisted its meaning according to how they want it to be, but, the truth about socialism remains the same.

Now, although Robert Owen and other socialists set apart the theory of socialism and presented it as something concrete that could serve as a foundation for economic systems, it is said that this concept existed from ancient times. Nevertheless, in the 1820s, Henri de Saint-Simon, an economic theorist, hinted towards this ideology when he acclaimed the ideal society as a large factory.

After his death, his followers invented a system in which the society could be controlled like a single factory, and they named this, socialism. Thus, socialism came into existence, giving people a new and beneficial perspective to life.

However, the question is, why was socialism created in the first place? The answer is simple: to establish and maintain a balance in society in such a way that poverty was eliminated. It was developed in opposition to the unrestrained behavior of liberal individualism and capitalism that occurred during the late 18th and 19th centuries. During this time, Western European countries experienced rapid growth in industrial production that some individuals and families rose to become rich while others descended deep into poverty, leading to discrimination and other social concerns. Thus, socialism emerged as the ideal economic system that could save a nation from many ills of society by simply establishing stability.

Why is Socialism a bad idea in today's world?

While at one point in time, socialism was a preferable economic system, it has now become a bad idea because of how the leaders have transformed it into something else. In addition, the state of the countries also does not allow socialism to be a beneficial economic system because of its many disadvantages.

The major disadvantage of socialism is that it counts on the cooperative nature of persons to work. It accepts those in society who are competitive rather than collaborative. As competitive individuals have a tendency to seek ways to overthrow and disturb society for their gain, they do not benefit society as much as collaborative individuals do. As a result, innovative people are not rewarded by a socialist society. Another disadvantage is that the government holds great power, and this has its own pros and cons. As long as it dedicates its goals and objectives to grant its people's wishes, it will be acceptable. Still, if the government does not attend to the citizens' demands, it will end up being a dictatorship regime like China, Russia, North Korea, etc.

Therefore, it's the government's responsibility to create a leveled platform to protect the rights of all the people in society and to work for their welfare and prosperity.

Now, as aforementioned, many socialist government leaders are not addressing the issues of the people in society but are instead, misusing their power. There is no equality anymore, as power and money have taken roots in those countries. We are living in an era when everyone is asking for equality. It was a request back in the day, which has now turned into a plea. Times have changed so radically that the poor have given up on ever gaining the justice and equality they deserve. They are not being rewarded well enough despite their efforts and contributions. All in all, leaders have forgotten their responsibilities towards the nation because of their greed for power. The leaders of socialist countries are living the lives of capitalists, while the rich are getting richer, and the poor are getting poorer. There is no one to address their issues, so they helplessly continue to suffer the consequences of the government's decisions.

Looking back at ancient times and comparing it to the world that we live in today, it is undeniable that we have progressed as a unit. However, it is imperative to remember that Socialism was initially founded to establish stability and balance in society on a personal level and not just on the whole. Today, socialist countries have entirely forgotten about the true meaning of the ideology that they adopted as their foundation.

Among the many aspects of life, powerhouse countries have especially been affected. Socialism has led to the destruction of the countries that once thrived. For instance, Venezuela's Hugo Chavez, which was praised for providing health care and education free of cost by stopping the United States' elitists from accessing the country's oil supply, has now gone bankrupt. The once-thriving country that had the largest reserves of heavy crude oil is now facing a shortage of food, utilities, and health care. As a result, more than a million people have fled the country, seeking asylum in other countries, especially the United States, with its booming capitalist economy. A couple of years ago, Spain was also flourishing and evolving from its previously underdeveloped state. However, they came under massive debt, and the taxes increased. The level of unemployment became unimaginably high, and everything went downhill. Nevertheless, these setbacks caused Spain to experiment with a socialistic governmental system with all its attendant problems.

Today, many people are trying to sell the socialist ideology to the American electorate but do not tell the people the whole truth. What they don't tell you is that socialism has destroyed many formerly thriving economies around the world.

Now while from a worldly point of view, this system is proving to be problematic on many levels, it is also hugely unacceptable if we look at it through the lens of religion, and this has been specifically highlighted through this book. The purpose is to unmask the true nature of practical socialism to the electorate, and particularly the youths on our university campuses. Socialist countries eventually replace God with their government.

Chapter 2
Educative Indoctrination

Socialism is becoming a prominent subject that needs everyone's undivided attention. Word of mouth is not enough to explain why and how we should consider socialism. This economic system started with one simple ideology in mind and went on to become a virus for countries that were already doing substantially well. It is on the rise in the United States of America and other Western countries. In addition, the people that are going to determine its implementation as the country's new system, along with the government, are the younger generation.

Many conservative parents still send their children to academic institutions to broaden their thinking and ethics, as it used to be decades ago. Unknown to them is the fact that nowadays most teachers in these institutions are left leaning. They are now brainwashing and indoctrinating the young students entrusted to them into believing a liberal ideology, particularly that socialism is the best system of government.

Subjects like politics, history, and other social sciences have been portraying socialism as an ideal government **system.** Of course, we all know that this is untrue, judging by the many countries whose economic system has been run aground by this failed ideology. Unfortunately, these students cannot challenge the professors because they are not well informed about the dangers of socialism.

The United States of America is considered one of the biggest countries among Western nations. They are the wealthiest nation and the most advanced both technologically and economically, and the leading superpower on the planet. They give financial aid to many developing countries. Many third world countries are inspired by the United States and its system of government because it works.

This powerhouse nation is now being threatened by the clamor for socialism by the Democratic socialist party. This could throw their established economic system horribly off track. Leftist politicians are now touting socialism as the solution for making America better than it is now. They are targeting the youth as the main group to lead this charge. Unfortunately, the youth have been so badly brainwashed that they are buying this lie hook, line, and sinker. It is a simple marketing strategy to get the youth on board and make achieving the objective easier. Fortunately, however, while the government aims at the youth for support, some of the students in major universities don't agree with it. According to those students, the professors and the politicians are telling lies about how this ancient system can be the switch that the country needs. They further go on to highlight that they are 'painting a rosy picture' about socialism and nothing else.

Some politicians that the country has held in high regard have already made the declarations for implementing socialism. One by one, more political individuals and experts joined in on the discussion and are in support of socialism. When someone with decades of experience speaks about the country's economic system, it must be something he has thoroughly researched.

The youth has been brainwashed for listening to the same things being said in favor of this system. Socialism is the same economic system that had destroyed flourishing countries in the past, which led to revolutions that we clearly remember until today. The reason that this has caught on the youth is that the proponents of the ideology promise free things to everyone, without talking about how to finance it. When someone comes and says that he is going to write off all student loans and give free money to people who may not like to work, people are going to want to listen.

Every professor is considered knowledgeable. They have attained intellectual power, and they have a degree to prove it. As a child, your parents told you that to reach your career goal, you need to do something remarkable. And to do something remarkable, you need to gather as much information as possible, and that is only with the help of the right coaches. The professors at a couple of renowned institutions are beginning to convince the younger folks that socialism can be the next big milestone that the United States can achieve with their help.

The only reason that the professors have taken such an upper hand on the lives of the students is because the parents were monitoring what was being fed to their children. Mostly those students agree with socialism whose information and exploration of the world were limited by their parents. According to a book by Lenore Skenazy, the students arrive on the campuses as young adults who have no idea of most important things around them. Since their parents restricted them because of their insecurities, the children give teachers the role of a parent. As a result, whatever they learn in colleges and universities will be the only information they will have about a subject.

Moreover, a couple of years ago, many students had their own politics reach extreme limits. This came as a result of students spending more hours on extracurricular activities on campus. Kyle Dodson, an assistant professor of sociology from the University of California in Merced, also confirmed that the students who are not engaged in classroom studies are more focused on building a career for themselves. They are the ones who are into violent political activities.

There are higher chances of leftist professors to be hired in an institution because of their role in brainwashing students to endorse socialism. Students will continue to experience indoctrination every single day until they accept it out of no choice. Eventually, they become a part of the liberal machine within the college. If you are considering a professor or any teacher as a parent and role model, you need to learn about them first. The parents are at fault for not paying close attention to their children and teaching them what they know. But when it comes to young adults, their decision-making quality should be good enough to see right through a person at times. If a professor is giving a lecture about socialism, the student must do separate research and match the teachings with what he has understood. Instead, the students are like sheep that are going to follow a shepherd blindly because he pretends to give them protection. It has everyone wondering how exactly the students are so attached to their teachers.

Another factor that comes into play during the academic phase of an 18-year-old is prejudice. Anywhere you may go, even at a new workplace, you will experience favoritism. It has been there in the world for centuries, and it is never going to go away. Nevertheless, favoritism or prejudice is not considered a severe problem these days because people choose to ignore it. While it works for them, nobody can force them to think otherwise. The same can be said for the idea of socialism. It is an obvious circumstance to be in because professors will teach what they do. Unless you argue with them by questioning their methods, they will continue planting seeds of deception in each student. When you are sitting in a class among students, especially the ones that are training to become socialists, you will eventually be left out unless you change your views. The reason students support socialism is largely due to its ideology of making the rich support the poor. Nearly half of the colleges around the United States have students that are struggling to keep their lives afloat. The developed countries have dramatically increased the cost of education. The students are working jobs to get some lunch money for the day or just save up for the fees of the next semester. It is not easy, and this is a major reason why students are tilting more towards socialism.

How many of you'll have been in that phase where you just wanted to get things to satisfy your desires? It is almost with everyone, and that is why our parents tell us that if we want something, we need to work hard for it. There is no other way to enjoy the rewards of hard work than to wait patiently for it and make the most of it. Socialism encourages a lazier approach to the hardworking scenario. Lazy is the key factor for students who have lost hope and just demand things after things, without any end. When there is prejudice on school grounds, you will immediately see groups scattered around. For a person that happens to pass by, seeing groups around the campus seems absolutely fine.

However, that person may never understand the tension and the circumstances around them. Friends will discuss the day to day matters in the light of the philosophy they espouse. That is enough to create the 'cool group' mentally around the campus.

In the 2016 elections where Donald Trump came out victorious, Hilary Clinton and all pollsters nearly had concluded that Hillary was going to have a landslide victory. As the votes started coming in, indeed, Hillary was looking like a clear winner until Trump pulled off a miraculous victory. The sole reason that Donald Trump won the election was that people were fed up with failed policies of the Obama era, featuring mass unemployment and terrorist attacks around the world, which seemed to have no end in sight.

Donald Trump, a highly successful real estate mogul, promised to change all that and ameliorate the sufferings of the common man. People believed him and decided to give him a try. His favorite slogan is that he was elected as the President of America and not as President of the whole world. He has so far kept his promises by putting the needs of Americans ahead of those of other nations.

Since the election of President Trump, America has made major strides both domestically and internationally. Since electing him into office, the following are some of his achievements within three years of his assumption of office:

1. President Trump's pro-growth policies are unleashing economic growth and providing opportunities to workers across the country.

2. President Trump is rolling back costly regulations that have burdened hardworking Americans and stifled innovation.

3. President Trump is negotiating fair and balanced trade deals that protect American industries and workers.

4. President Trump is rolling back costly and burdensome regulations to unleash America's incredible energy resources.

5. President Trump is expanding access to affordable healthcare choices and acting to lower drug prices.

6. President Trump mobilized his entire Administration to combat the opioid crisis that has devastated communities across the country.

7. The President is committed to defending the right to

life and religious liberty.

8. President Trump has made clear that his first responsibility is to protect the safety and security of Americans.

9. From the first day of his Administration, President Trump has worked to uphold the rule of law and secure our borders.

10. President Trump is rebuilding our military and defending America's interests across the world.

11. President Trump is restoring American leadership on the world stage and advancing an America first agenda.

12. President Trump is honoring America's commitment to our veterans by ensuring they receive the quality care they have earned.

13. President Trump has followed through on his pledge to transform the Federal Government and increase accountability and transparency.

Many of you will recall the Great Depression and how The New Deal series restored economic stability to the country. President Franklin D. Roosevelt introduced a series of programs to get out of the recession. Bernie Sanders is now erroneously claiming that this was a type of socialism. His argument is that if these programs by Roosevelt helped the United States recover from such a recession, socialism would be even more beneficial now that the country is better developed.

Progressives are brainwashing the millennials that socialism is the better economic system because it will redistribute wealth from the rich to the poor, cancel all student loans, and guarantee incomes for people whether they like to work or not. But we all know that this is a lie. During the Obama era, the credit rating of America was downgraded twice, and his government accumulated more debt than all previous presidents combined.

Added to this, the unemployment rate was very high. ISIS established a caliphate, and there was worldwide insecurity. All this was because Obama adopted a liberal policy with some tinge of socialism. Instead of creating jobs, he introduced several entitlement programs. He did not practice true capitalism. During his administration, China was on the rise as many US jobs relocated to China, and thousands of factories closed down in the US. If we go back to see how the Soviet Union and China under Mao Zedong's rule lived under socialism and see how today's countries have adopted it, we see there is no incentive for entrepreneurship in socialism. The latest country to adopt this system is Venezuela, and they hit the ground hard. It failed so miserably that it ran aground a once very prosperous nation. There was no economic growth, and poverty ravaged the land. People lost their businesses, homes, and life savings virtually overnight. The socialist government turned into a dictatorship as usual. Millions of Venezuelans had to flee to other countries seeking asylum.

The only reason that the demand by liberals for the failed socialist system rose was through a victory in the recent elections. Alexandria Ocasio-Cortez defeated a democratic congressional representative, and suddenly many liberals started to believe in an "improved version of socialism," especially the younger millennials. No matter what our politicians tell us, we should not forget that socialism comes with major costs. Anyone who has done some research about socialism will discover how mega socialist nations have crumbled to the ground. Now that many of us are aware of how bad socialism is, we must not allow such a bad system to destroy our great American dream.

Chapter 3
Socialism & Communism

The economic and political systems hold immense significance for any country as its citizens' progress and welfare depend on them. If this system is not controlled with wisdom and discipline, the country may end up being underdeveloped while gravely impacting the masses. The political and economic system controls production and trade concerning the government and its laws and customs. Goods are distributed within society, and prices are predetermined. Moreover, a set of rules and regulations is given to the manufacturers to follow so that everything may be done appropriately, and the country can progress.

Therefore, countries strive to establish a government system that is consistent with their values and beliefs. In pursuit of this, Socialism and Communism have emerged as two structures that have been widely embraced by countries in the past decades. As mentioned in the first chapter, socialism is solely based on public ownership, and the individuals depend on the government to provide food and health care. The government decides on the number of goods to be manufactured and its prices, not completely depending on making a profit. Instead, they focus on manufacturing goods for society to use, with no competition in the market. According to socialists, to establish equality in society, central planning and shared ownership of the assets must be carried out.

As for absolute Communism, this system focuses entirely on the betterment of the people of a society. It concentrates on being neutral when it comes to the distribution of profit after the production and keeps all property under the ownership of the community. Therefore, communism is also referred to as a classless system because of the methods that they use for the distribution of profit to provide every individual's needs.

The Differences & Similarities between Socialism & Communism

While communism and socialism are widely misconstrued to be the same, the truth is that they are not. There are many differences, such as its basic philosophy, planning of economics, ownership of economic resources, distribution of economic production, class distinction, and religion that differentiate them from each other. The biggest difference is the basic philosophy that relates to the distribution of wealth. When the time comes to distribute the profits that individuals gain from the production, the two systems are only slightly similar. In communism, the distribution of economic production and wealth is designed to serve the individual's needs. If there is a community that has rich people who are contributing more, the profit that they earn is distributed in such a way that people who do not do anything can benefit from it. However, socialism does not agree that those who are not contributing must benefit from other's hard work and effort.

The second difference between socialism and communism is the body that controls and manages the entire business of production. If you notice, now, every country abides by the laws of the government. As mentioned above, socialism has a central government to rule over members of the society; even the production is under their control. Communism leaves the decisions to be made by the community for everything related to their production. There is no central government to manage what they do, and they only intervene in important situations.

Another difference that they both have is ownership. The truth is that everyone wants to be the proud and satisfied owner of resources that can benefit them personally. In the communist system, this pride is not given any value as ownership is granted equally to everyone. The public owns the economic resources as a collective unit that establishes unity and balance. However, in socialism, individuals own personal property, and the government takes full charge of it.

The caste system and racial discrimination have always been a matter of concern in our society. Besides, financial inequality has also played a part in giving rise to discrimination, and unfortunately, the government is not addressing these issues. The rich keep getting richer while the poor remain poor, and even though the racial and financial inequality seems to be removed on the surface, it is still an underlying issue. Communism tackles this by abolishing the mere thought of castes or class system in the society. On the other hand, socialism has people who focus on earning more and having a higher position in society. This ignites the poor to rise in rebellion against the rich.

When we speak about rebelling against one another, our attention is likely to be diverted towards religion. History testifies to how people have fought to the extent of wars in the name of religion because of diversity. However, this diversity is bound to exist in society. There will always be people who do not share the same beliefs and values. However, communism does not establish this thought very effectively. It openly discourages the idea of having many religions in one society. Socialism, in comparison, welcomes its members to practice any religion they desire to practice.

Thus, while these two economic systems are different from each other, they still have a set of similarities. For instance, according to history, socialism and communism both resisted laborers' abuse by quite a few developed organizations during the Industrial Revolution in Britain. The Industrial Revolution marked an era where a big change in technology, culture, and other social and economic features occurred. During this time, both government systems accepted the deal, which stated that all merchandise and projects would be created by the government-controlled foundations or combined associations and not by private organizations. As a result, the focal government was essentially given charge of financial arrangements, including matters of free-market activity.

The Historical Background of Communism

The word 'communism' originates from the French word *'communisme.'* The French word is broken up into two Latin words; *'Communis,'* which means "of or for the network" and *'Isme,* " which reflects a state, condition, activity, or convention. Altogether, communism can be interpreted as "the condition of being of or for the network." Historically, this word was used to relate to different social circumstances before it began to be linked with more modern ideas of an economic and political association.

As indicated by an advocate of communism, Richard Pipes, the possibility of an awkward, populist society initially rose in Ancient Greece. However, in the 5th Century during the Mazdak development period in Persia (now Iran), communism proved to be a "revolutionary" attraction of colossal benefits. These colossal benefits were aimed towards the respectable classes and the Church for condemning the foundation of private property and for endeavoring to make a broad-minded culture. During ancient times, different socialist networks existed mostly under the motivation of Scripture. For instance, in the feudal Christian Church, some pious and religious people united their territory and property. Likewise, the thought of communism tracks back to the 16th Century, where an English essayist, Thomas Moore, wrote an article that influenced people's perception of socialism. In this article named Utopia, which was released in 1516, he depicted a community based on common ownership.

Within the span of two hundred years, different gatherings on the Roundheads during the English Civil War spread the redistribution of riches on the Levelers and the Diggers. They were the followers of William Everard. In the 18th Century, the French rationalist, Jean Jacques Rousseau, in his tremendously powerful Social Contract in 1762, laid out the reason for a political request. It depended on mainstream sway instead of the standard of rulers.

His perspectives proved to be persuasive during the French Revolution of 1789 in which different enemies of monarchists, like the Jacobins, upheld the redistribution of riches among the individuals. Nevertheless, the plot was recognized, and so, he was captured and executed along with a few other people. Despite this misfortune, the case of the French Revolutionary system remained a motivation for radical French scholars like Henri de Saint-Simon, Louis Blanc, Charles Fourier, and Pierre-Joseph Proudhon.

By the early 1800s, the libertarian ideas and the related thoughts of communism became broadly noticeable. This was because of the compositions of social faultfinders and thinkers in the French liberal circles. For example, Pierre Leroux and Théodore Dézamy studied the middle class and prompted a far-reaching intellectual dismissal of capitalism on both economic, philosophical, and virtuous grounds. Significantly, Philippe Buonarroti, one of Gracchus Babeuf's co-schemers, endured the crackdown on the Conspiracy of the Equals and composed a compelling book. It was titled, Babeuf's Conspiracy for Equality, and was distributed in 1828. His works and lessons motivated the early communist groups of the followers of François-Noël Babeuf, like the League of the Just, a Christian communist group led in 1836 by Wilhelm Weitling. This group later came together with the Communist Correspondence Committee in Brussels.

This merger of the two gatherings in 1847 shaped the Communist League, which was headed by German communist pioneer Karl Schapper. In the following year, Karl Schapper entrusted two founding individuals to compose a declaration. These were Karl Marx and Friedrich Engels. This declaration spread out the criteria of the new ideological group. In 1848, Marx and Engels offered another meaning of communism and published the term in their renowned leaflet called The Communist Manifesto.

The Communist Manifesto

The Communist Manifesto was initially titled as the Manifesto of the Communist Party and was translated by Samuel Moore. It was a political pamphlet that was released in late February 1948 and written by Friedrich Engels and Karl Max, two German philosophers. This document became known as the world's most influential political document.

The Communist Manifesto curtails Marx and Engels' thoughts concerning the idea of society and governmental issues. To be specific in their very own words, "the history of all up to this point existing society is the history of classic struggles." It also consists of their thoughts on how the industrialist society of the time would inevitably be ousted by socialism. At the end of this document, the creators talked about the "forcible overthrow of all current social conditions," which filled in as the legitimization for every single communist change around the globe.

After being in Manchester for two years due to employment in a factory that made sewing threads, Engels wanted to make his way home to Germany in 1844. Since he met his revolutionary partner Karl Marx before, Engels decided to make use of his stop in Paris to meet Marx, who was publishing a journal.

After meeting at a café, the two began developing a strong bond that lasted their entire lives. The two were working on a book that Marx had started, which was published a year after they met. By collaborating in the form of editing and writing, the two men developed a great understanding, which was visible in their breakthrough project.

We are highly fortunate to have their work available to us today. These parts of history will always be used for generations to come because of how effective they are in any era. It is more than 175 years, and their ideas have big political activists talking. Many writers of the 20th and 21st centuries have observed the Communist Manifesto's persistent relevance.

For instance, in a special issue of the Socialist Register remembering the Manifesto's 150th anniversary, Peter Osborne said, *"it's the single most influential text written in the nineteenth century."*

The editor of International Socialism, Alex Callinicos in 2010, said, *"This is indeed a manifesto for the 21st century."*

Moreover, probably the best review came in 2002 from an academic John Raines. He highlighted a point by saying, *"In our day this Capitalist Revolution has reached the farthest corners of the earth. The tool of money has produced the miracle of the new global market and the ubiquitous shopping mall. Read The Communist Manifesto, written more than one hundred and fifty years ago, and you will discover that Marx foresaw it all."*

Bolsheviks and the Russian Revolution

It was during the early 1990s that the most impressive imperial rule came to an end after centuries of dominance.

In just a couple of months, two events occurred in Russia, and one of them was the Russian Revolution. Although it was held on November 6, 1917, on the Julian schedule, it was October 24. Thus, it was known as the October Revolution.

During the Russian Revolution, Vladimir Lenin, the leader of the Bolshevik Party, led a group of people to try to overthrow a government that was led by an assembly called Duma. Duma ruled for 11 years in Russia, and they were formed by a congregation of leaders from the country's average class of capitalists. Lenin wanted a Soviet government that would be managed straightforwardly by committees formed by the army and laborers.

The Bolsheviks and their companions seized government buildings and other key locations in Petrograd. In doing so, they established a new government and made Lenin its leader. Consequently, Lenin became the head of the world's first communist state.

China Adopts Communism

The China that we know today was in a major conflict when the Qing dynasty ruled the land. During that time, the citizens saw an unbelievable rise in rent and taxes. The income generated from taxes went into the possession of the village chiefs and landlords. This resulted in two-thirds of the country being owned by 10% of the population.

In addition to that, they were also under constant attack by a fellow Asian country, Japan, that became a powerhouse by defeating Russia. China failed miserably to establish a stable government because of the defeat of the Qing dynasty. After seeing that there was no hope and improvement to rebuild what was once a powerful land, the leader was forced to seek asylum in the newly declared Asian powerhouse.

After years of trying to establish a solid system, the chairman of the Communist Party of China, Mao Zedong, led an army to help farmers reestablish their hold on agriculture. His goal was to redistribute the land by convincing the people that there was still hope, and Mao managed to get them to work with him. He led the people to fight against the government in the 1949 Civil War and defeated them. Consequently, China adopted communism and managed to get on the right track to stability. We cannot deny that without the inclusion of socialism in the world, we would never be witnesses to the other systems that derived from it. Communism was inspired by the many incidents that took place in the countries during the medieval times. These intellectual individuals whose names are mentioned in the previous and coming chapters were quick to point out and highlight the facts that could be improved to have a better place to thrive as a unit.

Famous Personalities of Socialism
ROBERT OWEN

In the first chapter of this book, I have mentioned the names of the people who were involved in creating the ideology of socialism. Among the many popular names that we know about today, Robert Owen is on the top of the list as he is one of the main founders of the cooperative movement.

Born on May 14 in 1771, Robert Owen worked was a textile manufacturer who strived to improve the working conditions of his fellow workers in the factory. He worked hard enough to become the manager of a large textile mill in Scotland. In 1817, Robert Owen began to implement the New View of Society, a system that he thought would prove beneficial as it became a crucial period in his life. He was so popular that the British government called on him for advice on how to eradicate the country's industrial apprehensions. Eventually, he became phenomenally successful in the regime, and it was proven in his textile mill. Hence, his strategy and motive to improve others' lives were noticed, especially in his efforts to promote social equality.

FRED C. HAACK

While Robert Owen was the first socialist, Fred C. Haack became the first-ever socialist politician in the United States of America. He was born in 1873 in Germany and became the first individual from the Social Democratic Party to hold open office in America. He was initially chosen for the regular board of Sheboygan in Wisconsin as an individual from the Populist Party in 1897. However, he joined in sorting out and managing the Social Democratic Party on a local scale. Running on the Socialist ticket, he was re-chosen as a councilman in 1898 and served a term of 16 years. Haack was perceived as the main American Socialist officeholder at the national show called the Socialist Party, which was held in Milwaukee in 1932. This was regardless of the fact that socialists had been chosen as Chicago councilmen and Illinois lawmakers since 1878.

MAO ZEDONG

Mao Zedong is and will always be one of the key figures in China's history. He led the people with his words and actions to live in a country that was slowly coming out of enormous debt and internal issues. However, Mao realized the need to keep up the system based on class for socialism after the revolution. The partnership between laborers was a key factor that should have been included in the financial base itself. Consequently, Mao set forward a line that puts a great deal of emphasis on the provincial masses. This was going to increase the demand for products of light industry and impact the heavy industry.

This method of improvement appears differently than how it was used in the Soviet Union in the 1930s. It brought about the pressuring of the lower class to give an enormous output, which surely allowed fast industrialization. However, besides that progress, it hindered the class principle of socialism and disengaged various sectors of the economy. All of this made the Soviet Union suffer, a situation persisting till today. Therefore, the contrasts between the Chinese and Soviet societies go further than just a question of 'who is and isn't aware of industrialist reclamation.' There may be concrete contrasts between the kinds of society the two nations were working on during their underlying times of socialist construction. Hence, it required an extraordinary nerve for the Chinese under Mao's administration to strike along an independent road.

XI JINPING

China is currently caught in a trade war with the United States of America, and therefore Xi Jinping will look to make use of every ounce of power that he has to make China stand a chance. The current Chinese President has called for socialism to defeat capitalism. There is no backup plan to compete with Donald Trump's America, who are seeing nothing but a comfortable walk-in-the-park like experience. For President Xi to manage the country's debt, he has to put a hold on the competition in the private sector.

China's new technique is floating the economy for the time being but undermining it in the long term. The government has fastened down on shadow-bank loaning to private firms and constrained many like it to close. Since Mr. Xi moved toward becoming director of the Communist Party in 2012, he has pledged an "extraordinary revival" to reconstruct China to its old unmistakable quality and wonder. Mr. Xi's way of thinking instructs that the objective of an incredible, united China can be accomplished if the Communist Party stand in solidarity for China. According to him, the assembly is the answer to China's issues, not their source.

Thus, capitalism may work for some countries, but it is not the system that every nation can afford to follow. One similarity between capitalism and socialism is that both systems consider labor and capital to be the main economic forces. China and many other countries like them are trying to reconsider using capitalism as its base to run an effective system. Therefore, the President of China is entirely confident that his decision to use socialism will regain China to be politically strong with its skill in technology.

Chapter 4
From Mao to Castro, the History of Socialism

Looking at the current state of the world, it seems like socialism is about to return. The trend all over social media is an alarming sign that we need to brace ourselves. Therefore, to address this, we first need to create awareness about how socialism is a dangerous virus that can sweep across any nation and destroy it from within. Today, if the people of the United States of America are questioned about their opinions regarding socialism or why they support it, it is expected that they will not have a clear answer to define the term.

This is because the socialism that the world knows today is nothing like the socialism that existed years ago. Therefore, we need to glance back at the lives of some great revolutionary heroes who dared to change the system of the country by embracing this government system. When discussing socialism, it is impossible to detach Mao, Castro, and Stalin from its history. These people were the communist heroes who saved the citizens from the path of devastation, although for a brief period. They had the power and authority to lead, unlike many other leaders of socialism who did not have the freedom to exercise their dictatorship. These people used extreme measures by going to the extent of conducting a war, but their purpose was solely to prevent their homeland from facing an economic depression. Nevertheless, due to their approach, they ended up becoming contenders of the Western powers.

In Russia, Joseph Stalin was known for being a scapegoat of the government's problems. He was one of the many names chosen to be blamed until he solved some major issues with his supporters. The people of the Soviet Union found him to be the perfect man to become the General Secretary. However, eventually, his strategy to rule instilled a fear in people as he did not spare anyone who opposed communism.

Fidel Castro did not only look intimidating with a compassionate soul, but his actions personified it. The Cuban led a force to topple a dictator and brought high-class values of health and education to the country. In the eyes of numerous people, he may be a saint who faced a superpower, but to others, he is a dishonest man who favored terminating squads for democracy. During his rule that lasted for five decades, Fidel Castro had thousands of Cubans imprisoned in horrendous jails, and some were denied fundamental political opportunities. Cuba made upgrades in the fields that mattered most but suffered due to Castro's harsh policies.

During the time of Maoism, a system named after Mao Zedong that focused on the small-scale trade and agriculture, China saw its power shift from property owners to the laborers. Again, for many, Mao is a hero, but even he made some errors that attract criticism. Mao's greatest botch was neglecting to do what needed to be done in the late 1940s. Mao had brought famine to the agricultural sector and left millions of people dead.

Moreover, he also deported all the intellectuals of the country. In 1950, an event in history known as Land Reform became the first impression that Mao made on the general public. This was one of the many activities that followed, which contributed to the progress of China. Mao Zedong unmistakably called for the citizens to pay attention to the current situation and focus on the future. A path was needed to be created for the Chinese revolution. That path was to experience the new democratic rule and advance smoothly into the phase of socialism. After the advent of the People's Republic of China, he created and continuously improved the socialist economic and political system by organizing a socialist economic, political, and social development on a large scale. Besides, he built up the institutional requirements, ideological certifications, and an authentic purpose for socialism with Chinese characteristics. This became an ideal external condition to construct China's socialist development.

During this procedure, Mao began a progression of hypotheses about China's socialist development. He proposed to accomplish the second blend of the generally accepted fact of Marxism with China's resources. Mao also wanted to do it according to China's particular manner and find a way of structuring socialism that suits China's national conditions and embraces its values. Mao also made an extraordinary hypothetical commitment to the historical backdrop of China's socialist improvement.

His thoughts gave adequate ideological growth and the ideal arrangement for the second significant jump in Marxism's sinofication. They served not only at the initial stage of the history and settlement of socialism with Chinese attributes but also as one of China's core values of transformation, development, and change. Mao's investigation left us with an experience of accomplishment and lessons learned from errors, both of which empower us to accumulate substantial experience and significant motivation for the present development of socialism with Chinese characteristics.

After studying the historical and theoretical points, we can easily conclude that Mao turned out to be an extraordinary founder and discoverer of the reason for socialism in China. China has been the quickest developing economy on the planet since the 1980s. After the rule of Mao in 1978, China has been progressing from an overwhelmed state of the organized communist economy to a unified market communist economy. This change required a complicated number of amendments in China's budgetary, management, and legal bases. Moreover, it needed the capacity for the legislature to have the option to react adaptably to the unplanned outcomes of these changes. This change has been added along with great amounts of industrialization and urbanization, which have influenced each part of China's public life, culture, and economy. Thus, since the time of the financial change that started in 1978, China has seen an incredible improvement in the standards of living and has experienced social stability and consistency. From that period, China has advanced from a disengaged socialist state into a backbone of the global economy. While they have concrete systems now, back then, they had to go through two of many economic hardships. Those two significant efforts were the First Five-Year Plan in 1953 and the Great Leap Forward in 1958.

China's Five-Year Plan

The Five-Year Plan is an outline that nearly every country implements as it sets a list of economic targets for it to achieve in the next five years. This list is later evaluated to see how the missed objectives can be completed in the years following that. When it came to China's list of goals to achieve after the country was founded, it released its first list in 1953. Apart from that year, China did not manage to release its plan from 1963 to 1965. The objective of China's first Five-Year Plan was to take a shot at a high-pace economic development and stress upon the improvement in the heavy industry. The heavy industry included fields like mining, iron assembling, and steel assembling. In addition, it also wanted to improve on technology like machine development as opposed to agriculture.

To accomplish the first Five-Year Plan's list of objectives, the government decided to go with the Soviet model of economic improvement. According to this model, it underlined fast-growing industrialization through investment in heavy industry, as mentioned above. Thus, the initial Five-Year Plan used the Soviets' style, which revolved around state ownership, cultivating groups, and centralized economic planning. Although the Soviets helped China make its Five-Year Plan, it was not appropriate to China's economic conditions. In that era, China was technologically deficient, with a high proportion of individuals in comparison to assets. Plus, the government did not fully understand this issue until 1957.

For the first Five-Year Plan to be as effective as possible, the Chinese government had to nationalize the industry to focus on the capital for heavy industry projects. While the USSR co-supported a significant number of China's plans for the heavy industry, they helped China by funding them financially, which was expected to be paid back. To develop capital, the Chinese government nationalized the financial system and used oppressive taxation and credit strategies to pressurize private entrepreneurs to sell their organizations or convert them into publicly-privately owned businesses. In 1956, there were no private organizations in China, and other employments such as handicrafts were unified into cooperative organizations. This arrangement to support heavy industry worked, and the production of metals, concrete, and other mechanical merchandise was modernized. Numerous manufacturing plants and offices were also opened. In doing so, it increased production by 19% every year between 1952 and 1957. Similarly, the industrialization of China expanded laborers' salaries by 9% annually during this time.

China's agricultural business was not accorded much importance. Nonetheless, the Chinese government attempted to make agriculture more modernized as it did for private companies. The government urged farmers and plot owners to collectivize their farms. The decision of collectivization enabled the government to control the cost and distribution of agricultural products. They decided to keep the food costs low for urban laborers, but it didn't expand the grain production as considerably as they expected. Despite allowing the farmers to pool in their resources at that time, the families were permitted to own a little portion of land. By granting this privilege, the families were able to grow crops for their own consumption. This step enabled 93% of farmers and their families to become part of the system.

The Great Leap Forward

In Chinese history, the Great Leap Forward was the crusade attempted by the Chinese socialists between 1958 and 1960 to engage its vast population. The reason that it aimed at large-scale rural communities was because it had to deal with China's mechanical and farming issues. The Chinese planned to create a vast strategy for industrialization, which would promote the workforce instead of machines and capital consumption. Consequently, there was hope that the nation could elude the usual and increasing industrialization procedure by gathering capital and buying heavy industrial machines. The Great Leap Forward was demonstrated by the advancement of little backyard heaters made from steel in each rural and urban neighborhood. It was expected to quicken the industrialization process. The proclamation of the Great Leap Forward was the consequence of the disappointment of the Soviet model of industrialization that China adopted. The Soviet model, which stressed the conversion of the capital gathered from the selling of rural items into heavy machinery, was unsuitable in China. This happened because, in contrast to the Soviet Union, China had an exceptionally large population but not a broad agricultural foundation from which they could gain capital.

After a prolonged discussion, it was decided that farming and industry could be created simultaneously by changing individuals' working habits and depending on the workforce as opposed to machine-focused modern techniques. Right from the beginning, an investigative group was set up in the north-focal area of Henan in 1958, and the framework, before long, spread all through the nation. Under the cooperative framework, rural and political choices were decentralized, and ideological perfection, as opposed to skill, was emphasized. The laborers were divided into unit groups, and shared kitchens were set up with the goal that women could be liberated for work.

The program was executed with such scramble by persistent units that particles were regularly liquefied to make steel in the furnaces and unhappy workers butchered many farm animals. These blunders in execution were intensified by a progression of cataclysmic events and the withdrawal of the Soviet model. The carelessness of the group and an illogical approach towards the practice of agriculture greatly unsettled China's farming system. It took three long continuous periods of regular cataclysms that immediately led to a national catastrophe. Altogether, around 20 million individuals were estimated to have died from starvation in 1959 and 1962.

This breakdown of the Chinese economy compelled the government to withdraw the Great Leap Forward program by 1960. Private plots and agricultural resources were given back to the workers, expertise started to be emphasized once more, and the joint system was separated. The failure of the Great Leap created a division among the chiefs. One group claimed that the failure of the Great Leap to bureaucratic mechanisms came at the hands of those who felt overly enthusiastic about executing its strategies. Another group in the party took the failure of the Great Leap to be proof that

China must depend more on expertise and material motivations in building up the economy. Some inferred that it was against the last group that Mao Zedong propelled his Cultural Revolution in 1966. With everyone blaming each other, the country was left hanging and in dire need of a miracle.

After the events of the Great Leap, China decided to look for a new way out of their misery. With communism and Mao's failing vision, a member of the Communist Party suggested that a new economic system should be adopted. Hence, in 1979, Deng Xiaoping and then President of the United States of America, Jimmy Carter, signed a treaty, agreeing to end the tension between the two nations.

Deng took full responsibility for making China greater than before, and he did that by launching several economic reforms. With the help of it, private sectors commenced and operated businesses on their own like they were doing before. This was one of the significant steps that Deng had taken, including establishing four zones where the country could attract and benefit from some foreign trade. These reforms enabled China to come on the road to recovery and eventually embrace a free-market competition that they once hoped to have.

Stalin – A Social Democratic Labor Party Leader

If we had to decide who qualifies to be the world's most cruel leader, it would be hard to choose between Iosif Vissarionovich Dzhugashvili and Adolf Hitler. Losif Dzhugashvili, or better known as Joseph Stalin, was a Georgian revolutionary and Soviet politician who led the Soviet Union as Secretary-General of the Soviet Union and Premier from the mid-1920s until 1953. The meaning of Stalin was 'man of steel,' and this was displayed in his character.

Stalin was born into a low-class family. His mother was a washerwoman, and his father was a cobbler. However, he did not have a happy childhood as his father was a heavy drinker who continued to punish him physically every day. Nevertheless, his mother stayed with him, instead focused on raising Stalin never to become a man like his father. As the young Joseph grew up, Georgia and its sentimental old stories and antagonistic Russian conventions caught his creative mind. And so, even though his parents had sent him to become a priest, Joseph chose another path for himself. The upbringing and only goal that was set by Stalin's mother was to convince him to go into priesthood. Instead, he rebelled and pursued the mysterious compositions of Karl Marx and joined a nearby communist gathering. He dedicated quite a bit of his opportunity to the progressive development against the Russian government and soon lost enthusiasm for his academic pursuit. Conflicting with his mom's desires, Stalin turned into a non-believer and began competing with the ministers. He was thrown out of school for failing to appear for the tests, which made him more rebellious from a young age.

The study of being a socialist and his enthusiastic approach to revolutionary activities was the center of Stalin's life. While he worked as a clerk, Stalin continued to organize protests and strikes. As he strived to be a notable figure in Russian history, he decided to join an underground party called the Bolshevik. Six years after Stalin joined the party, he robbed a bank to fund a project where he conducted guerrilla warfare in the Russian Revolution. Stalin became a famous hero when he became a significant helping source for Lenin, the leader of the party he joined. He voiced his opinions and organized the Russian Revolution. In this revolution, Lenin vowed to bring peace, land, and bread to the Soviet Union's citizens. Besides being by Lenin's side, Stalin helped him escape into Finland by freeing him from an army. With that act of bravery, he was appointed to a position of command in the party, and that is when he ordered the deserters of the civil war to be killed immediately. The Russian Revolution was a success, and Lenin appointed him as the General Secretary of the Communist Party.

A couple of decades later, Lenin suffered a hemorrhagic stroke and died. The next person who gathered all the authority to himself was none other than Stalin. He played smart by having his rival to the seat exiled for criticizing Stalin's plan of solidifying the country. The party changed their minds about the vision Stalin had, and he was handed the power to the Soviet Union. This reign brought rapid industrialization but an increased paranoia that ignited the infamous purge. It was akin to doing ten good things while also doing five bad things. The people were happy under his rule but equally terrified.

Another person with a similar philosophy and approach to leading a nation like Joseph Stalin was Fidel Castro. Born on August 13, 1926, Fidel Castro was a democratic revolutionist and was well-known for overthrowing Fulgencio Batista, a person he knew very well. As mentioned before, Fidel Castro had a significant influence on progressive politics by jailing protesters, and he survived many assassination efforts. In addition, he also provided free education and healthcare to the public.

Like the above-mentioned names, Mao and Stalin, Fidel Castro also received mixed reactions for the things he did. As one of the few individuals that changed the landscape of their homeland, Fidel Castro is still respected as a person. He did everything to put his life on the line for its prosperity. After his death in 2016, the entire country mourned for nine days. During his funeral, people all around the globe sent in their tributes and condolences, except the current President of the United States of America, Donald Trump, who decided to keep the decades of rivalry between America and Cuba alive. Trump tweeted in a criticizing tone and making it clear that Castro brought suffering and nothing else.

These three titans incorporated the socialism infrastructure in their countries. While seeing the state of the people and the economic and political system, they had to take a stand to bring order and control. There was no doubt that they were cruel dictators, but it cannot be denied that their countries benefitted from their rule in the long run. Lives were sacrificed and used as an example to others for going against the laws that were enacted.

Chapter 5
The Gentle Socialists

A country stricken by recurrent dictatorship is bound to face destruction no matter how developed it has been. All it takes is one poor decision made by the leader, and the entire economy bears its consequences. The period of recession and depression turns into a vicious cycle, and the general public suffers.

Mao's rule over China, Castro's rule over Cuba, and Stalin's rule over the Soviet Union also led to the economic decline of their nations. On paper, they seemed to have a firm grip on politics and resources, but they lacked consistency. Many times, they ran out of solutions and lost hope, and this led these leaders to choose the path of war. It was an extreme way to exercise power in their country, but it worked. However, today, no country would choose war to solve economic issues. In the previous chapter, we learned how things could turn out if dictators are socialists. We learned about Mao, Castro, and Stalin and their socialistic approach to governance. We also learned that despite the uncertainty of progress and the devastation caused by war, their efforts to achieve their goals proved to be beneficial for the people of that time. Today, China, the Soviet Union, and Cuba have become definite followers of socialism because of their leaders' influence. They have used guidance from the Marxist-Leninist model to build the country's politics. According to previous reports, approximately 27 countries established themselves around these ancient principles of socialism. Since then, only a few nations still use it except for China, Cuba, and the Soviet Union, who, after being victims of war and destruction, chose another direction for themselves.

Meanwhile, some countries still follow socialism, but they are not as extreme. Bangladesh, India, Guyana, Nepal, North Korea, Tanzania, Sri Lanka, Venezuela, and Portugal are some famous socialist countries. With the help of the democratic approach, these countries have brought about discipline and stability in their economy.

A country must create stability in such a way that the needs of the people are efficiently met, and the issues are effectively resolved. If the country does not come up with proper solutions for common problems, it will inevitably face a decline. This may include issues like unemployment, strikes, poverty, or all the above. Therefore, it must be a priority to eliminate the possibility of backwardness by ensuring stability in every way. Today many countries stand as examples of how stability can bring a country out of backwardness into a state of development.

A recent study on countries practicing socialism has shown a big loophole. It has been observed that the countries' socialistic practices suffered enormously. Therefore, it is essential to clarify what we should expect from socialism. These countries had acres of land under their control and were also considered superpowers back in the day.

Therefore, they were likely to experience civil and international wars and the overthrow of governments. Back in the day, people did not understand the meaning of Marx's theory. So, the countries took advantage of it and declared themselves as socialist countries even though their practices differed from Marx's beliefs. The same is true for government systems today. We cannot assume that the leaders are adhering to the ancient socialistic values as the world has become more technologically advanced now. Therefore, they have drifted away even more from the original idea of socialism, which is one of the many reasons the systems are failing today. The countries have misunderstood socialism and have molded it into what they want it to be. The desire to establish a better economic and political agenda left Stalin, Mao, and Castro with no other choice than to impose extreme measures on the country without realizing its true danger. Every system needs to be managed based on the amount of resources and industries it has. If the country is forced into a system that does not keep within the limits of its resources, it can result in a disaster.

Therefore, we need to educate the new generation about the adverse consequences of the extreme version of socialism on nations and their people. Nations must practice only such government systems that are good for the future of the nation and its people.

However, several countries were lucky enough to see their glory days after they became independent. This is irrespective of the acres of land they occupied or the number of the population they had. That may sound irrational and unbelievable, but Venezuela is a typical example.

Those that know about Venezuela in the 21st century can see how severely they are suffering from economic problems. But decades ago, the country went through probably their best period in its history. After they had been detached from Spain, they did not have to start from scratch, as some may expect. Venezuela was not affected severely since it focused on its basic practices of economic and political policies. The country stood its ground withstanding future wars and rotational governing power.

Besides the instant progress of third-world countries under socialism, the world was shocked to see how taxpayers were building a place where education and healthcare were free, and there were improved living standards. This progress was by courtesy of the Nordic Model, which was an advantage that many ancient countries did not receive but still survived independently. The Nordic Model attracted more people to invest in foreign trade and led the country to become one of the Western powers. Norway, Denmark, and Finland are some states that have implemented this agenda, which has made these countries a great place to live in and where people can trust the government and join hands with them to overcome challenges.

Venezuela was not far behind if we had to compare its situation in the early 1900s to the Nordic countries. If there is a country that has oil as its economic resource, it would not need any backup supply to increase opportunities for foreign earnings. Therefore, Venezuela's oil reserves became an object of envy for other countries. Thanks to the oil reserve, the country's GDP was recorded as the highest in Latin America in 1935.

However, it was not all fun and games, as this useful resource also led to an increase in the country's crime rate. Dictatorship continued in Venezuela for ten years after establishing high numbers in Latin America's evaluation of GDP. The system was toned down temporarily under the new President, Isaias Medina Angarita, as he brought in the political party idea and many other reforms to bring more stability to the developing country. Then, in World War II, people from Europe immigrated to expand the society and made it more diverse.

The civilian-military groups were the ones that kept taking turns in ruling Venezuela. Romulo Gallegos defeated Romulo Betancourt, who took charge courtesy of the coup in the fair elections. It was the first time when the country had taken the step to hold free elections to determine its next President. This began in 1945 and went on until 1952 when Perez Jimenez came at a time when the state's economic condition was weak. In his rule, he made it even worse. Venezuela's growth was limited because the government interfered in the private companies, causing it to stop its overall growth. It was now a country based on capitalism, and it made various businesses step away from the regime. This happened just when the government was on the brink of collapsing.

Because of the debt that Marcos Pérez Jiménez had left the country with, an amendment in the financial program became crucial in Venezuela. The Economic Recovery Plan of 1960 came forward as a comprehensive approach by Tomás Enrique Carrillo Batalla. The development business was renewed through the "re-discount" of the Central Bank of Venezuela, and the Economic Recovery Plan fulfilled its goals. In 1964, Venezuela received the option to come back to a secured conversion scale with the free trade of foreign money. The framework continued until the Venezuelan Black Friday of 1983, even though the model was at the point of running out toward the ending years of the 1970s.

The solidification of the fair democratic agenda and the dispersal of fears of political radicalization of the nation, standardized the interest for foreign money, balancing out the parallel conversion scale.

For a significant part of the period somewhere between 1950 and 1973, the Venezuelan economy was characterized by its stability and continued durability. These factors contributed conclusively to have the option to keep up a fixed swapping scale without real burdens. In the time of Carlos Andrés Pérez, his first time as President, because of the Arab-Israeli war, better known as the Yom Kippur war, the average cost of a barrel of oil went from $3.71 to $10.53 and kept on ascending to surpass $29 in 1981.

The salary of the open segment went from 18,960 million bolivars in 1973 to 45.564 million in 1974. The financial jackpot additionally had the attributes of an appropriate economic system, yet Venezuelans recollect the "Ta barato, woman dos." That was a war cry that translated to "It's very cheap, give me two." The expanded inflow of assets to reserve funds, loans, and mortgage banks permitted an expansion in the loan portfolio, which equally tripled. All in all, Venezuela was a prosperous nation in the administrations of Rómulo Betancourt, Rafael Caldera, and Carlos Andrés Pérez. In 1975 the iron business was nationalized, and the next year the oil business had a name. Thus, Petróleos de Venezuela, SA (PDVSA) was established. The election of Carlos Andrés Pérez in 1973 clashed with an issue about their oil trade, in which Venezuela's pay detonated as oil costs took off. The oil businesses were nationalized in 1976.

This prompted considerable increments in public expenditure. However, the debts increased around the same time, which proceeded into the 1980s when the oil costs collapsed and affected the Venezuelan economy. As the government devalued the currency in February 1983 to confront its budgetary commitments, the Venezuelans' lifestyle deteriorated significantly.

Various bombed financial approaches and expanding degradation in government prompted a rise in poverty, unlawful activities, and expanded political instability. Oil costs tumbled from $120 per barrel to $9 per barrel and after that bounced back to $40. They would not go anyplace close $120 once more. This constrained the government to cut imports, which was hard because Venezuela did not create any income-generating resources other than oil. The nation depended solely on imports to get food, medicines, vehicle parts, etc. But, when the imports were cut, famine struck the country. To handle this, the government attempted a few things. One, they showed double trade rates. This procedure gave businesses dollars to import products that were regarded as the basis of economic stability. Everybody mishandled this arrangement, including businesspeople and administrators in government. They would lie that they were bringing in primary products, only to sell them on the black market at much higher rates.

There was a massive problem in health care as Venezuela suffered a decline. Fortunately, there was still hope for some countries because they moved towards an agenda called Medicare for All. Concerning the current period, people frequently pointed to nations with substantial social projects. The best examples of this system are Canada, the United Kingdom, and the Nordic states, especially regarding human services. Even though they are not very dedicated socialist nations, they possess profoundly highly taxed markets with enormous welfare programs. Besides that, they offer a government-assured healthcare delivery system that many countries, including the United States of America, do not offer. The issue for their contention is that apart from working on improving these charitable projects, a portion of the nations are seeing a continuing development of private medical insurance. Medicare for All is the noticeable socialized medicine proposal in the United States and is identical to the Canadian structure, in which suppliers charge the provincial office that oversees the program. In Medicare for All, there are no cost-sharing plans, and every service is provided conveniently. It includes professionally prescribed medications, dental, vision, and other services that are considered necessary by the secretary of health and human resources. However, patients must wait long in line to see a doctor.

The frameworks of those countries and their Medicare for All programs are similar in the sense that they use provincial workplaces to oversee repayments to suppliers. However, they vary in basic ways because they use cost-sharing for specific services. They are less far-reaching in their coverage, and they consider the private medical coverage that intends to supplement or enhance the system. This would cover 'out-of-pocket' costs and evade delayed periods to get access to specialists. These are unmistakably the things Medicare for All would resolve. It's fascinating to point out that while socialists in America would race to nationalize the health care services, Norwegians, Swedes, and Danes are, on the whole, bit by bit expanding their utilization of private medical coverage. Somewhere in the years between 2006 and 2016, the part of the population secured by individual protection grew by 4% in Sweden, 7% in Norway, and 22% in Denmark.

The increments in Sweden and Norway are not too remarkable, yet they are significant. This is by considering that most out-of-pocket payments have a moderately low yearly limit. Private plans in Sweden and Norway are intended to enhance the administration run plan.

Besides taking care of out-of-pocket costs, these plans certify prompt access to unique or elective strategies, often failing when the state plans it out. Denmark additionally permits "give-and-take" insurance plans. These plans cover various services and are mostly under any conditions secured by the national agenda, including dental and vision administrations.

This developing European enthusiasm for private medical coverage ordinarily originated from disappointment with the state-run agendas. They frequently gave inadequate or deficient services and long postponement periods. Ironically, individual plans offered more extensive services with shorter postponing times, access to private accommodations, and greater adaptability in patient decisions. For example, in a review released in 2009, almost 50% of Danes felt the postponement periods were preposterous, whereas just about a third opposed this idea. In 2007, the Danish government approved a waiting time assurance of one month to get treatment.

The more significant part of the private medical coverage in Denmark, just as in Sweden and Norway, was based on employee selection. In Denmark, the expansion in private insurance was likely because of a limited extent. The employers or bosses tried to enroll top-level individuals by including a well-being benefit as a significant aspect of a helpful bundle. Thus, private safety insurers made a solid pitch to managers, educating them that having individual benefits limited their workers' time that is lost to sickness and guarantees they had brief access to medical care. Also, in that 2009 review, the biggest part of respondents believed the most significant factor of employer-based coverage was that it brings about being "less absent due to sickness because of snappier treatment."

The second and third most well-known reactions were that it gave access to private clinics and reduced long waits in the open framework. Along these lines, private options provided an incentive for ordinary Danes who were getting premium health services as an advantage of the business. It was also attractive for Danish bosses who could vie for the high part of the arrangement showcase, and for the backup people who were selling this service.

Private protection plans were also attractive for the government since they reduced the number of people depending on government insurance. Generally, 50% of respondents in the study had their last medical clinic visit paid by a private safety net provider. This would all be illegal under Medicare for All, and individual medical coverage would be nullified for everybody. Danes are on the right track to deny that they are a communist nation. However, their liberal welfare programs and those of the Swedes and Norwegians are objects of envy for American communists.

While the other human services frameworks are also extraordinary in their specific conducts, they all offer widespread inclusion for their respective citizens, and any cost-sharing comes with low yearly restrictions. They give about everything that an advocate of socialized healthcare could do. Nevertheless, every one of these nations has a developing private medical coverage sector.

The American leftists grasp a stage that keeps on looking increasingly more like a communist fantasy. They claim that the case of Venezuela is the bad dream of communism. A typical reaction from the left is that communism, or popularity-based communism, works fine and dandy in Sweden, Norway, and Denmark. It is undoubtedly clear that Sweden, Norway, Finland, and Denmark are prominent monetary triumphs. What is false is that these nations are especially socialist.

To the degree that the leftists need to point to a case of fruitful socialism, not merely generous welfare countries, the Nordic nations are an unfortunate case to refer to. The fact is that the Nordic nations practice free-market economics and couple it with high charges traded for liberal government qualification programs.

Adding to the point above, the reason many believe that these are not socialist countries is that the wealth is not generated entirely from administration benefits but also from private firms. This wealth helps liberal government programs. Unions are sensibly amazing in many ventures and arrange contracts, but the government does nothing to guarantee a specific result from those dealings. Laborers are paid according to their wages, and these are not settled by the government's view of what is fair. The government gives families vouchers for every child. These vouchers can be utilized to go to customary state-funded schools, government-run contract schools, or private and revenue-driven schools. The utilization of government assets to pay for private and revenue-driven schools is something contrary to socialism.

Socialism can appear as government controlling or meddling with free platforms, nationalizing businesses, and financing favored ones. The Nordic nations don't do a lot of those things. They offer government-paid human services like health care, and sometimes the educational cost is free. College fees and other liberal social security nets are all financed with high taxes.

It is conceivable to do these things without meddling in the private sector more than required, as this will help organizations become profitable. It delivers the high corporate and individual wages that help the tax collections, making the benefits by the government doable. The Nordic nations will never be keen enough to murder the goose that lays the golden egg.

Chapter 6
The Unsung Hero – Capitalism

Millions of youngsters today expect a lot from the government. Having these expectations is not wrong for people who pay taxes and have appointed the government to run a system that benefits the people. The more a common man dives deeper into the regime and the culture, the more he realizes their future is uncertain. Every youngster worries about his or her savings before the time they retire, but not everyone has developed a mindset to save.

According to a report in 2018 that CNN released, nearly 66% of youngsters have nothing saved for their retirement. These youngsters' ages ranged from 21 to 32, and the reason for ignoring the purpose of saving was that they were uncertain about the economic system lasting long enough until their retirement age. Their reason is rational enough to a point because time changes a country's system. Still, it is not concrete enough to justify the longevity of the current effective system, which is capitalism.

But what is capitalism? It is one of the most common terms that has been used along with socialism over the past two years. Therefore, what really is capitalism, and why is everyone talking about it?

"Capitalism" is derived from the word "capital," which itself comes from the Latin word "caput," which means head. With this system, money is the head. It characterizes capitalism as an economic system where a nation's industry, trade, and benefits are constrained by privately owned businesses, rather than by the individuals whose time and work control those organizations. The United States and many countries around the globe are industrialist-based nations. Capitalism is one method by which it may settle the issues of economic production and distribution of resources. Rather than arranging monetary choices through brought-together political techniques, similar to those of socialism or feudalism, financial planning under this economic system happens through decentralized and intentional choices.

The most flawless type of capitalism is laissez-faire, a system that practices free-market methods. Here, people belonging to a private firm are given a free hand on how they want to run their business. They can figure out where to invest, what to produce and sell, and at which costs to trade goods and services. The laissez-faire system works without checks or any controls. However, most nations practice a blended framework of capitalism that incorporates some level of government guidelines of business and responsibility for selective industries.

Just like socialism and communism, capitalism also has its set of pioneers that helped people and governments evolve gradually to adapt to this effective system. Two people come to mind, and they are Ludwig von Mises and Adam Smith. I think without influential people like them, we would never live in nations like the United States or Nordic countries, where this economic system would be implemented and benefit us.

The Mises and Smith Effect: Pioneers of Capitalism

Ludwig Von Mises is one of the few notable individuals in capitalism as his lessons are important to the preservation of material civilization; he showed that its base is the division of work. Without the higher profitability of work made by the division of work, the incredible greater part of humanity would just go extinct because of starvation. The presence and productive working of the division of work imperatively rely upon the characteristics of a society founded on capitalism. These characteristics comprised a restricted government and financial opportunity, private ownership of lands and other properties, trade, investment and saving, monetary disparity and competition, and the motive for earning profits have affected the establishment everywhere for ages.

At the point when Mises showed up on the scene, Marxism and the other socialist-inspired organizations were delighted in imposing a virtually intellectual business model. Real defects and irregularities in the works of Adam Smith and David Ricardo and their followers empowered the socialists to guarantee vintage-style inspired economics as their genuine partner. The works of Jevons and the early Austrian market analysts, Menger and Böhm-Bawerk, were inadequately thorough in giving a compelling counter to the socialists. Frédéric Bastiat had attempted to give one but unfortunately died too soon, and most likely came up short on the essential theoretical insight anyway.

Consequently, when Mises showed up, there was no efficient intellectual restriction to socialism or the defense of capitalism. In a literal sense, the intellectual walls of civilization were undefended. So, Mises attempted to assemble an intellectual protection of capitalism and civilization, and that outlined the main reason for his greatness.

The main argument of the socialists was that the foundations of capitalism served only the interests of a bunch of tough exploiters and monopolists. Furthermore, it worked against the interests of the incredible dominant part of humankind, which socialism would serve. The main answer others offered was to develop plans to remove the business people's riches as the communists were requesting. The other option would be to encourage property rights to be regarded despite incongruence with the vast majority's prosperity.

Mises tested everybody's fundamental opinions by showing that capitalism works in the material personal matters of all, including the non-businesspeople. In a capitalist society, Mises showed that the market is served by privately owned means. The physical donors of the plants and factories are people who purchase those items. Together with the aim of profit and loss and the opportunity of competition that it suggests, private ownership guarantees a consistently growing supply of items for everyone.

In this manner, Mises appeared to disagree completely with clichés like "poverty causes communism." He clarified that it was not just poverty but also the mistaken idea that communism is the solution for poverty. He showed that if the misinformed leftists of the declining nations and of devastated ghettos understood financial matters, any desire they may need to battle poverty would make them capitalism promoters.

Adam Smith, the Father of Economics, became famous for his pieces known as The Wealth of Nations and The Theory of Moral Sentiments, which were released in 1776 and 1759, respectively. He has defended this way of organizing human affairs on good even-minded terms, which overturns centuries of religion-based warning that one ought to maintain selfishness. In Smith's view, seeking one's interests to the general lack of concern about what happens to outsiders is vital to national success. A free and commonly helpful exchange makes a superior showing of guaranteeing the general welfare of the state than generous sharing or charity. Adam Smith assumed that people were self-serving. However, if everyone were to look for the satisfaction of her or his own personal interest, the material needs of the entire society would be met. Hence, there was no requirement for the government or any outside power to meddle with or attempt to control the market. Privately held property and profit would be the standard and added help in achieving this would be the motivating force.

Society might profit if there were no business models or monopoly so that rivalry could work, according to Adam Smith. For instance, on the off chance that one baker in your neighborhood charged $10 for a loaf of bread, he would not get away with it as long as another baker was willing to sell his bread for a lower price. You, keeping your best interests in mind, would go to the less expensive baker.

We call this competition. Furthermore, for instance, one individual owns most of the pastry shops in your neighborhood, and he raises the price. You would have no other choice except to have to pay or go home buying nothing. We call this a monopoly. Adam Smith, as mentioned in his book, calls this inclination for the competition to keep the prices of items under the requirements of customers the "invisible hand." The invisible hand of the market will enable everyone's personal interest to accommodate the general interest of society.

Adam Smith similarly illustrated the possibility of a 'division of work.' Productivity is significant in an industrialist economy. Adam Smith observed a pin manufacturing plant and said that pins could be produced more effectively only if "one man draws out the wire, another straightens it, a third cuts it, a fourth points it," etc. A larger number of pins could be created and delivered by following this strategy than if one individual made the entire pin each time. This was the introduction of the modern-day industry.

Both intellectual individuals admired and respected the opinions of other people like them. They both liked when Ludwig showed appreciation and admiration for Adam Smith's work by saying,

"Smith's books did not lay the foundation stone, but the keystone of a marvelous system of ideas. Their eminence is to be seen precisely in the fact that they integrated the main body of these ideas into a systematic whole. They presented

the essence of the ideology of freedom, individualism, and prosperity, with admirable clarity and in an impeccable literary form.

This ideology blew up institutional barriers to the display of the individual citizen's initiative and thereby to economic improvement. It paved the way for the unprecedented achievements of laissez-faire capitalism. The practical application of liberal principles multiplied population figures and, in the countries committed to the policies of economic freedom, secured even to less capable and less industrious people a standard of living higher than that of the well-to-do of the "good old" days. The average American wage-earner would not like to dwell in the dirty, badly lighted, and poorly heated palatial houses, in which the members of the privileged English and French aristocracy lived 200 years ago, or to do without those products of capitalist big business that render his life comfortable.

The ideas that found their classical expression in the two books of Adam Smith demolished the traditional philosophy of Mercantilism and opened the way for capitalist mass production for the needs of the masses. Under capitalism, the common man is the much-talked-about customer who "is always right."

The above-stated words were from the introduction Ludwig gave in 1953 to Henry Regnery Co. Ludwig was greatly inspired by the Father of Capitalism's work in "An Inquiry Into The Nature and Cause of the Wealth of Nations." Many capitalists, including the people of today's generation, use these two as their inspiration for founding a capitalist system in developed countries.

This system is already on the rise, with people like Donald Trump being at the forefront. But how did he come to know about this specific system that made people so passionate about seeing it in their countries?

Origins of Capitalism

The fundamental subject of capitalism is the utilization of riches to create more riches. The foundations of capitalism stretch back to the 16th century. This happened when the powerful British systems had crumbled to the ground after the Black Death. The Black Death was a dangerous disease that killed up to 60% of Europe's population. A recently founded group of dealers started a foreign exchange initiative with foreign nations. By the 18th Century, England had changed over into an industrial country, and the beginning of the Industrial Revolution saw a blast of manufacturing overtake the island. It is within those smoky industrial facilities and combustible material factories that the innovative thought of capitalism started to blossom. This freshly discovered interest in exports hurt domestic economies and led to the creation and pricing of products. The downside of this was that it prompted the spread of colonialism, oppression, and imperialism.

Capitalism brings about the best items at the best costs. That is because the purchasers will pay more for what they need the most regardless of the size of the item. Organizations and companies offer their customers the products they need, and at a price that they are willing to pay. It keeps the costs low by rival brands in the fair nature of competition while making sure of the quality of their products while at the same time ensuring profitability. Most significantly, economic development is capitalism's inborn reward for advancement. This encourages innovation and technological advancement.

No wonder then that the thriving countries of today like China and some Nordic nations have applied this to their welfare system.

China's Rise After The Great Famine

Decades after the Communist Party took control in 1949 in China and promising to serve the individuals, the greatest manmade calamity in history struck and effectively ruined the land. In a city in the Henan region inhabited by millions of people, starvation and cruelty took the lives of one of every eight citizens during three painful years.

In one region, the authorities took more grain than the farmers had really cultivated. Within a period of nine months, over 12,000 individuals, or 33% of the population died, and a tenth of the families were wiped out.

Thirteen youngsters desperately requested the authorities for food and were driven deep into the mountains, where they died of starvation. A young orphan murdered and ate her four-year-old sibling. A town of 45 residents lost 44 of its members, while the only survivor, a 60-year-old woman, lost her mind. Others were tormented, beaten, or buried alive for refusing to surrender what little food they had. The whole country had been run aground. That was when Deng Xiaoping stepped in after Mao Zedong's death in 1976. Following Mao Zedong's demise, Deng outdid the late administrator's picked successor, Hua Guofeng, in December 1978. Due to social clashes, disillusionment with the Communist Party, and other institutional issues caused by the incoherent strategies of the Mao period, Deng became the principal figure of the "second generation" leadership via party.

Deng opened China to outside investment and the worldwide market. This turned China into one of the fastest developing economies on the planet for more than a few generations and raising the way of life of several million. This has been credited to his Open-Door Policy of 1978. This policy allowed the Eastern countries to gain access to trade with China, which proved to be very beneficial for the country to recover from the disastrous past.

With countries as powerful as the United States and Japan taking an interest, Zeng was close to bringing China's glory back, and he had to focus on economic reform in agricultural supplies. Deng Xiaoping started his program of financial change in the countryside, where workers were urged to partake in the market economy. Cooperatives and communes were destroyed and were split into plots of land that was rented back to laborers who were urged to raise yields to sell in private showcases.

In the late 1970s, the cooperative framework baffled Chinese farmers, who considered it restrictive to the improvement of both the agricultural establishment and their lives. The changes started with the "household contract" and "responsibility system." The project won Deng's support and was immediately executed across the country, making it a huge breakthrough in economic reform.

Later, the "responsibility system" ended up becoming widespread all over China, and incentive cost rewards for the above-production limit grain creation were presented. Many have said that Deng set up a framework that permitted the Chinese to excel at making money. The early economic reforms implied that individuals could earn money selling products at neighborhood markets and doing work at home. Mending garments or fixing pots and creating independent ventures were some examples. While Deng Xiaoping never held office as the head of state, head of government or General Secretary, people called him "the architect" of another brand of reasoning that joined a socialist philosophy with a capitalist one, whose motto was "socialism with Chinese attributes."

Israel Under Capitalism

The erupting of the Israeli-Palestinian clash in the mid-2000s caught most specialists off guard. The 1990s ecstasy of the Oslo peace process was suddenly shattered and replaced by a subsequent terror. The newspeak of 'harmony profits' offered an approach to banter about imperialism. And, rather than 'worldwide village-ism,' there is much talk about the war on terrorism. Interestingly, most academic, and popular experts appear to see this emotional change largely as a chance event.

In a world overwhelmed by postmodern narrative and talk, nothing is sincerely genuine. On the other hand, the main truth is the thing we see on television and read in the papers. As per the media, the Israeli-Palestinian clash, like all disputes, involves ethnicity, religion, and culture, and these factors have their good and bad times. The prime leaders like state authorities, armed forces commanders, otherworldly figures, and religious icons of such feelings are pioneers of different sorts whose conflicting urges produce various results. In the present combination, Israel's far-right driven by Benjamin Netanyahu and Ariel Sharon activated the move from harmony to war. They shredded the delicate Oslo Accord to proceed with the settlement of Greater Israel. Tragically, so far, there has been little effort to go past these prompt appearances. History positively is openly finished, yet it isn't irregular. In addition, keeping in mind that ethnicity, religion, and culture are genuine highlights of our entrepreneurial world, they can't satisfactorily clarify its advancement.

Israel is a capitalist nation in a capitalist world, and along these lines, its history, including its contention with the Palestinians, should be arranged inside the more extensive procedures of capitalist advancement, locally and globally.

"If you want to understand the way an economy works, there's one book you need to read: The Road to Serfdom."

A former prime minister of Israel said these words to a young supporter. The prime minister is Benjamin Netanyahu. He was not fully successful in getting Israel to the level of stability that is stated in the book, but he provided growth to the country that nobody expected. During his tenure, the country has its shareholders and taxes reduced, with the GDP increasing over 5% in his first term of presidency.

Israel's grip on the free market is especially remarkable because it is one of the main places on earth where socialism once had a level of achievement. The nation's religious mission and wartime balance directly from its introduction to the world created an uncommon financial history. The little durable population made successful plans for changing a desert to agricultural land while building crucial combat hardware firms. Most early pioneers worked on aggregate homesteads. The government-controlled almost all capital, and private organizations ordinarily were expected to request the government for resources.

For a period, the outline worked. Persuaded by the injury of the Holocaust and some energetic vision, early farmers accomplished something near the aim of aggregate ownership. Financial requirements and social issues soon drove second-generation Israelis to restore private property and convert most farms into genuinely customary so-called specialist organizations. Israeli socialism came smashing down in the mid-1980s when hyperinflation, powerful associations, and gigantic inefficacies numbed the economy. A progression of seriousness assessments coupled with increasing loan costs balanced out the circumstances. However, Israelis rose out of the tax issues and low standards of living for everyday comforts comparable to other technologically propelled popular governments.

During the 1990s, things started to change. Upon his rise to the prime minister's post in 1996, Netanyahu cut taxes and started to change the economy. High-pay workers have seen their expenses drop over 20%, and about half of Israelis pay no taxes at all. Revised labor laws have additionally started to take control of the nation's once-predominant associations. Actions to streamline government organizations have made it simpler for private ventures to raise capital and open their doors. Finally, a few large state-owned organizations have offered shares to the public. All in all, the change has worked.

After a good extension during the 1990s, Israel's financial development topped the graphs in the evolved world for the most recent few years. Inflation is under control, and the size of the government has decreased as compared to the economy. Once-abandoned streets are currently packed with chic boutiques; there is another airport, new streets, and new offices.

Nordic Country Chooses Capitalism Over Socialism

It is amazing how many people think one of the main Nordic countries is a great example to follow for the United States of America to become socialist. Sweden is one of the handfuls of countries that have tried socialism and is using capitalism as their economic system. Many individuals have a big misconception about Sweden because the country itself realizes that socialism can never work out.

Most would agree that Sweden was a socialist state at any rate regarding personality and the heading of public policy. In 1975, Sweden's state possessed well over half of the profitable assets in the nation and organized the costs of the rest. It subsidized debt by having high assessment rates with generous deductions for borrowers. Its actions at "Keynesian" policy interventions were unwieldy, confused, and made dangerous vulnerability in investment returns even in those parts of the economy that were still market oriented. The state heavily taxes thriving businesses and uses the returns to subsidize projects that were wasteful or falling flat. This implied that loan interests on capital were restrictive, particularly when double-digit inflation is applied. To protect laborers, the state insisted that wages couldn't be cut, and implemented a series of limitations on ending cutbacks, and different methods for altering hours.

Luckily for its residents, yet tragically for the individuals who think Sweden is a socialist country, the Swedish government, pretty much by all-inclusive accord, turned forcefully back toward capitalism starting around 1995. It liberalized the local industry, privatized its educational and pension agendas, as well as opened the economy to universal exchange and competition. The reason it did this is absolutely because capitalism consistently produces success. Most areas are unregulated, and the opportunity to move capital makes Sweden among the most industrialized countries on the planet.

There has been a lot of discussion regarding taxes. Sometimes countries cut them down, and sometimes they increase them depending on their economic stability. Regardless of their decision to balance their system, there will always be taxes. However, some countries have high taxes to generate more revenue, provide healthcare benefits, balance budgets, and carry out wealth sharing. The Northern European countries are receiving all the benefits that are stated above, with healthcare being the biggest reward. However, in some states, overall economic growth is drastically retarded. Back in 2010, Ohio had an enormous unemployment rate. Obama tried to balance things out, but it still left 27,000 Ohioans without a job. There was a huge argument, and as of today, it has come down to 4% from 10%.

There are many ways that high taxes, which are a trait of socialism, can affect the economy. With the taxes increasing, businesses can't afford to pay the wages, and their extra efforts go down the drain. The prices of products go up; it leads to inflation, which many countries have seen over the years, and some of them are currently going through the phase. Moreover, the quality of the product diminishes as the funds to improve it are not sufficient.

Besides the dwindling number of jobs, necessary resources become unavailable, and this is where the citizens suffer, while the government is benefiting from its raise.

Chapter 7
The Flaws of Marxism

Marxism is an economic and social system that is dependent on the political and financial theories of Friedrich Engels and Karl Marx. Since it is a way of living, it is difficult to explain everything about it. The name Marx is familiar to every socialist and communist today. His theory of Marxism is summarized in the Encarta Reference Library as "a theory in which class struggle is a central element in the analysis of social change in Western societies." Encarta was Microsoft's creation for a digital multimedia encyclopedia from 1993 to 2009.

Marxism is the direct opposite of capitalism, which is characterized by Encarta as "an economic system based on the private ownership of the means of production and distribution of goods, while capitalism is characterized by a free competitive market and motivation by profit." Marxism is the system of communism where the overwhelming element is the public control of methods for production, distribution, and trade.

Under capitalism, the lower class is the regular, hardworking people with the ability to work on something specific and sell their own work and services to consumers. As per Marx, a class is characterized by the relations of its individuals to the methods of production. He declared that history is the sequence of class battles, wars, and uprisings. Under capitalism, the laborers are paid an absolute minimum amount of money, which is enough to feed their families. The worker is distanced because he does not influence the work or item that he produces. The capitalists sell the items created by the laborers at a proportional value as compared to the labor that was involved in making it. Surplus worth is the distinction between what the laborer is paid and the cost for which the item is sold.

An expanding economic impoverishment of the low class happens as the aftereffect of economic recessions. These recessions result because the average workers can't earn the full result of their labors, and the authoritative capitalists don't consume the majority of the surplus worth. As a result, a working-class or socialist revolution may happen, where the methods by which the ruling class forcibly keeps up course of action over different classes is a dictatorship of the lower class, as indicated by Karl Marx. Communism advances from socialism out of this movement. The motto is, "From each as per his capacity, to each as indicated by his work" for every socialist. The communist slogan "From each as per his capacity, to each as indicated by his needs," varies in this way.

Marxist perspectives on religion were that since the laborer under the capitalist systems was hopeless and estranged, religious beliefs continued to provide relief to the believers that they would be rewarded in another life. According to Marx, religion was the reaction to the agony of being alive and the reaction to earthly suffering.

"Religion is the moan of the mistreated animal, the sentiment of a wanton world, and the spirit of callous conditions."

Marx gave the above statement in his book titled, "Critique of Hegel's Philosophy of Right" in 1884. In this writing, he further demonstrated that the regular workers, the lower class, was a genuinely revolutionary class who was widespread in character and familiar with all universal suffering. This gave the need for religion to be continued.

Just as everyone has their own valid reasons for wanting to do certain things, Karl Marx had an ideology that went entirely against private properties and the decision to let most of the countries accept capitalism. Private property is the material foundation of freedom. Having a property makes the individual independent economically and frees the mind and body from dependence on others. When the person is independent, he or she will be more confident to voice opinions and stand against dictatorship.

Private property rights and human rights are quite similar and inseparable. Regardless of the economic system currently being practiced, those that control the private property of others control the lives and deaths of those individuals. One of the members of the Communist group, Leon Trotsky, explains it very clearly. He says,

"In a country where the sole employer is the State, opposition means death by slow starvation. The old principle, who does not work shall not eat, has been replaced by a new one, who does not obey shall not eat."

The idea of property started to take shape when man turned into a producer. He started to develop the soil so he can use it to plant and harvest, manufacture tools, and elevate production in anything. The question came to his mind, "For what reason should I share the rewards for all the hard work with my uninterested neighbor slouching in the sun?" That question has resounded through many generations. The fair distribution of the produce is the focal issue of social association and of a justified social order.

Obedience and compromising to earn bread and butter for oneself and the family is applied to the importance of having private property. When you possess something that is yours, you are not answerable to anyone about what you do, unless you break the law of the country. It became one of the reasons why Marx wanted this ideology abolished once and for all. When one seizes private property, he seizes that individual's will to live and gain control of the future, which could lead to starvation, as Trotsky stated.

Besides affecting mental health, the abolition of property rights destroys freedom, where it begins to jump-start a moral breakdown. This moral breakdown brings social chaos and the worse side of dictatorship. John Adams said that the moment people find out that property is not as sacred as God's laws, and there is no force of law or justice protecting it, mayhem will rise.

Karl Marx accepted that all property is obtained by power or blackmail. He also had faith in the unrest and that the takeover of property are the main path to social improvement. As times have demonstrated, with the abolition of private property, human opportunity, morals, and equity are gone. Socialism's absolute dismissal of property rights is reflected in its all-out amorality and upside-down moral concepts.

Power is the biggest weapon for an individual living in any society. Many people, especially young people, want to have as much power as they can to live in a state that fulfills their purpose. Many of the nations in the world have surrendered themselves to living under the government's power, which is one of the norms of socialism. Countries are struggling to develop long-term strategies for their stability, but people are still siding with the fact that socialism and government rule is better.

The previous chapters have a detailed summary of the countries that had socialism in their regime and what happened to them. They saw some positivity during that time, but their depression phase affected them to the point of no return. In fact, it is safe to say that they were saved with the right leadership at the right time. But this means that most of the people of America want to avoid the incidents that led people to flee socialist and communist countries or kill themselves to escape the hell they were living in.

Today's socialist countries adopt a centrally planned economy where the government has control of all the means of production. Under a genuine socialist system, it's the government's job to decide output and pricing levels. The real test is synchronizing these choices with the needs of buyers. For example, socialist financial specialist, Oskar Lange has contended that, by reacting to stock levels, central organizers can maintain a strategic distance from significant creation of wasteful aspects. So, when stores experience an overflow of a commodity like tea, it flags the need to cut costs.

One of the claims of socialism is that the absence of competition between various manufacturers decreases government authorities' motivation to cut costs. The critics also claim that public control of production fundamentally leads to a wasteful organization. A similar central organizing board could be responsible for regulating many items, making it incredibly hard to respond to market signs promptly. However, there is one plus point to take away from the government's rule. That point is that those who are sick or become too old to work can seek help from the state. The government is responsible for providing them with whatever they can. Some prefer it because when older people retire, they receive a pension. This pension becomes a regular payment in the form of gratitude. It also applies to disabled people and is commonly implemented for those who have served their countries, such as people in the military and the navy. The families of veterans also receive care from the government after their deaths.

Speaking of deaths, you may have learned how brutal the medieval era was. People kept dying a lot because they had no other option to free themselves from the misery of their country. Under the Marxist theory, not thousands but millions of people lost their lives. According to the numbers from the Black Book of Communism, China recorded 65 million, the Soviet Union had 20 million, Cambodia and North Korea had 2 million each, Vietnam and Eastern Europe had 1 million each, Africa had 1.7 million, and Latin America had 150 thousand estimated deaths.

According to one witness of this era, the initial issue was that it went all wrong when the communist ideology insisted that man must exist only for the sake of the state. When we think about these words now, it does seem like a hard principle to abide by, especially when it leads to nothing but unfair means. Things like methods, decrees, policies, promises, and details are all forgotten when we adopt socialism.

This reason is more than enough to bring everyone's attention to the evils of socialism and to oppose this evil ideology as a population. Young people, even below the tender age of 10, an age where they were supposed to be free from all sorts of worries and enjoy life like there is no tomorrow, saw their world and their country fall apart before their eyes.

Deaths increased in numbers, and there was nothing anybody could do to stop it. My advice to all young people is to reject the lies and indoctrination of politicians and professors, whose main desire is to rob you of your liberty and freedom. Parents should take more interest in knowing what lies are being sold to their children and debunk them so that these impressionable minds who are the future of the country will not be ideologically hijacked by socialists and Godless people. The socialist and communist economic and political system does not value human life, and they position themselves as the God of the people. All their pursuit is about power and control. There are millions today who lived under socialist and communist regimes that will clearly tell you that both are the worst ideas anyone could have come up with. Sadly, some Americans, especially the adults, seem to have forgotten the destruction these ideologies have brought to humanity.

Where Marx is the one to blame for all of this, he was blinded by the bright image that was put in front of him by G. W. F Hegel. Marx never discerned the innate danger, nor did he clarify how socialism would really emerge after the destruction of capitalism. Also significant is the fact that he never at any point undertook to find out how the state would fade away after the dictatorship of the working class started. Marx's philanthropic foolishness did nothing to dissuade Lenin from announcing, "Liberty is so precious that it must be rationed."

Marxists accepted that tremendously expanding government power was the best way to freeing humankind. Admiring order and control was the reverse of slandering costs and benefits. Nevertheless, every powerful system rapidly progressed toward becoming a flop in themselves.

In 1932, Josef Stalin proclaimed that the punishment for any burglary of state property would be death. As many Ukrainians were starving because of the severe collectivization of farms, even children robbing a couple of ears of corn could be shot on sight.

Marxism vowed to end the class battle but did so only by oppressing nearly everybody. Abolishing private property left individuals prisoners to authoritarian government authorities, who snubbed any individual who refused to kneel before them.

Socialism and Communism are still frequently portrayed by either ill-informed or deceitful individuals as ethically better than capitalism. They claim that under capitalism, companies keep on exploiting individuals for benefit. In any case, Eastern Bloc systems turned into a huge burial ground for Mother Nature as well. Pollution was unavoidable to a great extent because of the idealization of economic gains.

For whatever length of time that the manufacturing plants thundered and the output of steel rose, it did not make any sort of difference if individuals and everything else were perishing.

Marx never planned for his doctrines to spike everlasting fear in hundreds of millions of exploited people. On the other hand, it was criminally unsuspecting to expect positive outcomes from any structure that conferred unlimited power on rulers.

Under the capitalist system, people are fined and charged for going against the law. When people break the law, they are made to pay according to the severity of the offense, and everyone is comfortable with that. But under a repressive regime, the people need to think twice about doing anything wrong, even if it is unintentional.

Repression includes different activities to limit certain gatherings associated with social or economic activities.

Marxist thoughts focused more on the political rather than economic issues. Enough time has passed since the downfall of the Soviet Union to enable Marxist models to flourish without responding in due order regarding socialist systems.

In any case, the way that each socialist nation in world history immediately transformed into a severe bad dream is somewhat significant.

Marxist governments stomp all over individual rights since the Marxist theory could not care less about individual rights. Marxism is a theory of class equality. The main political rights it regards are those practiced by individuals from the persecuted class, with various left-wing ideological strands characterizing those classes in terms of monetary, racial, gender, or all at the same time.

In contrast to liberalism, which considers rights to be a positive good that can grow or contract for society all in all, Marxists, as well as other left-wing pundits of liberalism, consider political rights as a lose-lose struggle instead of a 50-50 one. It could be possible that they are practiced for the benefit of mistreatment or against it. Any Marxist government promptly starts snuffing out the political privileges of parties or ideas that are considered reactionary, more specifically a class that additionally poses to depict any threat to the forces that be. Repression is woven into Marxism's ideological fabric.

It is safe to say that Marxism failed miserably. It was designed to wipe away poverty, something that everyone wants in this world. The individuals know how hard they are supposed to work for the betterment and contribution to society. This system only grew in popularity because, compared to the United States, the Soviet Union had a low unemployment rate during the 1930s. Although it was designed to remove something as chronic as poverty, it was going to be corrupt.

It does not take long for anyone to violate the system, and that is what happened with Marxism. The officials in charge became greedier as Marxism took full control of the state and made sure that the people suffered. They gave no incentive to the workers that work for them, so they lost their motivation to work and do anything to get the job done. While working to create a paradise to live in, it forgot about those that are working hard to achieve that goal. Moreover, the negative side of it is that it looks like it is impossible to implement in the real world.

Chapter 8
The Democratic Socialists

The world has witnessed many changes taking place over the years. Some are lucky enough to see it and call it a curse. As people begin to learn more and dive deeper into the factors that cause these changes to take place, they also try to come up with a parallel outcome. It is a distinct possibility that during that phase of economic and geographical changes, not everyone knew what caused it and that a particular issue would trigger such an outcome. If they did, they would have taken a stand for it, but like in many tragic events, it was too late.

The 21st Century people recall those stories when they were told about their grandparents suffering in the same land they live in. It brings in an attitude that is desperately needed to think about a new strategy to stop it from affecting the current generation. While some of us are still wondering what method will be more productive, some politicians have already laid out their plan to the citizens, and in no time, a revolution begins.

Every citizen understands the importance of a country's political and economic system's well-being to be preserved and improved with time. For that to become possible, there needs to be someone who has witnessed or knows about the most effective systems inside out, including how it must be implemented. Bernie Sanders is a politician who believes in the same system that once nearly wiped out some of the Western powers.

Not everyone knows the history of Bernie Sanders as much as the Americans do, but he is one of the veterans in the political system. He is a 78-year-old American politician, who is considering bringing in socialism to take the United States of America to newer heights.

Bernie Sanders was born to Jewish parents of Polish descent in the Flatbush territory of Brooklyn, a borough in New York. He later married a fellow government official named Jane Sanders, a political consultant with whom he has four children, three of whom are stepchildren and one biological child. Just like every other American, his parents encouraged Sanders to attend Brooklyn College before gaining a bachelor's degree in political science in 1964 from the University of Chicago. While he was still residing in

Chicago in 1963, Bernie Sanders engaged with the civil rights movements, eventually becoming part of the 'March on Washington.' After some time, Bernie Sanders lived on a kibbutz, a collective community based on agriculture, in Israel after successfully graduating from Chicago. He returned to the United States and participated in public back-to-the-land development. He filled in as an association artisan and independent journalist. But his work did not stop there.

He additionally took an active part in the anti-Vietnam War movement, which drew him into electoral legislative matters. Running as an Independent, Bernie Sanders made several unsuccessful attempts for Governorship of Vermont in the years 1972, 1976, and 1986, as well as in the U.S. Senate in 1972 and 1974. Then in 1981, Bernie Sanders was elected mayor in his hometown. Although it was a narrow victory, he proved to be the ideal man for the job as he stayed in power for eight years. Before Bernie Sanders became a member of the U.S. House of Representatives in 1990, he lost twice. However, after being in office for only a year, he labeled himself as a self-described democratic socialist. He also joined the Democrats and became a rival of the then-president of the United States, George W. Bush. As the years passed, Bernie Sanders continued to build his name in the political world by being known for his socialist ideology. He voted against the Iraq War and opposed tax breaks benefitting only the wealthy people and corporations.

These decisions led Bernie Sanders to be reelected more than five times, and each time he won by a large margin. However, his most significant achievement was when he won the U.S. Senate race in 2006 and continued his campaign to improve tax administration the following year. Furthermore, nearly five years later, he gave one of the most memorable speeches in the history of the United States. He spoke for nine long hours in a speech now titled as, "The Speech: Historic Filibuster on Corporate Greed and the Decline of Our Middle Class." In this speech, he clearly explained why he did not agree with George W. Bush's tax cuts and why he was serious about his self-proclaimed title as socialist.

In George Washington University in 2019 and Georgetown University in 2015, during a bid for the Democratic presidential nomination, He further cleared the case of the title when he defined democratic socialism.

"If there was ever a moment when we needed a new vision to bring our people together in the fight for justice, decency, and human dignity, this is that time. Today in the second decade of the 21st century, we must take up the unfinished business of the New Deal and carry it to completion. ... We must recognize that in the 21st century, in the wealthiest country in the history of the world, economic rights are human rights. That is what I mean by democratic socialism." (Vox.com)

On the one hand, Bernie Sanders made his speech sound like the ultimate motivational talk that America needed to adapt to socialism.

On the other hand, Donald Trump is running a state that supports capitalism. Nevertheless, this did not make Sanders change his vision for America. The only thing that has changed from the similar speech he gave in 2015 is the environment and circumstances around him. Back in 2016, Sanders was going up against the Democratic Party's corporatist wing. However, in 2019, he faced a foe in the form of a government led by Donald Trump, known as Populism.

As much as Americans want to debate, there is an element of fear and fascination regarding the reoccurrence in the effort to bring socialism to the country. The fascination comes from the younger generation that wants to see a system that favors them, but the elders fear this change, as they know very well about the disastrous consequences.

The speeches may have caught the attention of nearly every American, but Bernie Sanders still created a couple of loopholes in the process that not everyone noticed. This resulted from not fully understanding the history and meaning of the word 'socialism.' I am writing this book to debunk the lies some politicians are telling about how great socialism is and prevent the electorate, especially the young generation, from being misguided.

While Americans may think they know what Bernie Sanders is talking about, the history of the affected countries shows otherwise. As I mentioned in the previous chapters in this book, the developed countries have made great strides to get to where they are today. Socialism is a word that is used imprecisely by the citizens of the country, including every Sanders follower. Therefore, many Americans are yet to be convinced about bringing socialism back. They find nothing convincing about why Bernie Sanders considers it the only way for America to excel and still be competitive with other world superpowers. In one paragraph, Bernie Sanders talks about the country. He speaks about how it should not come under any kind of stress because of its durable welfare regime.

"Are you truly free if you are unable to go to a doctor when you are sick, or face financial bankruptcy when you leave the hospital? Are you truly free if you cannot afford the prescription drug you need to stay alive? Are you truly free when you spend half of your limited income on housing, and are forced to borrow money from a payday lender at 200 percent interest rates? Are you truly free if you are 70-years-old and forced to work because you lack a pension or enough money to retire?"

Not only is this a typical leftist critique of capitalism, but it also holds a significant part of the power it had back in the times of Karl Marx. Sanders is advocating for free healthcare for both legal and illegal residents, socialist policy for the financial industry, and liberal old-age pensions. While that might sound like a compelling point to bring in socialism at the time, the only problem was that he did not talk about the ways by which the concealment of free markets has more than once created another type of oppression over the past century. If someone had interrupted Sanders when he said that, people would have thought twice before giving their undivided attention to him.

Bernie Sanders is just one of the many advocates of the socialist movement. None of the socialist advocates ever mentions the fact that socialist regimes not only nationalized large parts of the economy, but they also destroyed any hopes of freedom. They have made it impossible for people to engage in free trade and usually abuse their power to get rid of their rivals. The dictators made the same decisions to get the upper hand during their implementation of socialism.

Instead of speaking about the disadvantages of the system that he is advocating, Sanders continuously criticizes the system that Donald Trump is implementing. According to Bernie Sanders, Trump's order was the same one that began the demise of America. He further clarified it by making references to two names that included Adolf Hitler and Benito Mussolini in the autocratic regime. As he did that, he misled many people to support him. However, while those two dictators practiced some form of capitalism, he left out individuals like Mao Zedong and Joseph Stalin, who amended socialism and made their respective countries see the worst times in their history. By ignoring these important names, Sanders fooled many Americans into thinking his plan was perfect. The speech that was given was a typical rant against the opposition, which was Donald Trump in this case. It was all about one party trying to denigrate the other by pointing out the flaws and disadvantages of their agenda.

There are still some people who are against Trump, and Sanders tries to get them on his side by painting a false picture of socialism. Hence, the entire anti-Trump supporters have become part of this potential move. By saying that Trump is no different from autocratic socialists like Richard Nixon and John Boehner, Sanders is distorting the truth and is hiding the fact that true socialism has inevitably led to the collapse of nations' economic systems where it has been practiced.

Medicare is arguably one of the most important services any government should provide for its citizens. Its main objective is to spur a significant change in the way we pay for and manage healthcare services in the United States. Regardless of whether the MFA moves toward becoming one of the nation's laws, the surrounding discussion is increasingly vigorous. Politicians of various ideological persuasions are clamoring to be a part of the history-making changes to the decades-old flawed healthcare delivery system. Every American is conscious of the decline in the current healthcare system, as 14% of the adults keep on being uninsured regardless of the Patient Protection and Affordable Care Act. But those that have insured themselves find it exceedingly difficult to pay for the care they desperately require.

Life expectancy and infant mortality are some problems that the citizens of the United States of America face. That is even though the country spends double on healthcare than any other country in the world. The best approach to solve this problem is to turn to consumerism and market competition. This means that people will be able to shop across state lines for the best bargains. In doing so, the competitors will be forced to reduce their prices.

Dictatorship was one of the many preferred strategies that Karl Marx proposed when he wanted to brainwash the people to end capitalism. According to his theory, the workers had to be freed from their capitalist way of thinking as well as the environment in which they were born. This was to be achieved by a self-appointed political hero that would educate the people against false capitalist consciousness. That hero was a dictator, and he will tell the people how to think, associate, and act in the best system that humankind needed, which was socialism.

Countries like China, Cuba, and the Soviet Union were the best examples of failed socialism. Mao, Castro, and Stalin were each involved in the downfall of their respective countries that made every other nation oppose socialism.

- Mao brought famine to the agricultural production that left millions dead, deported intellects, and brought in reforms that brought instability to the country.

- Fidel Castro became one of the most hated and loved persons in Cuban history. He was loved for bringing in socialized healthcare but was hated for being a dictator who believed in killing his opponents and jailing people for not following his harsh policies.

- We knew Josef Stalin for being a fall guy of the government's evil doing. He was one of the few names chosen to be blamed because of his popularity in the public eye. That was until he took a stand against his people and killed every one of them through his followers. The citizens of the Soviet Union found him to be the perfect individual to become the state's General Secretary, but his way of ruling made people fear him because he did not spare anyone who deserted communism.

These three dictators were part of a very few leaders that had power like that during the reign of socialism. Some people remember them as heroes, and some as villains. They brought amazing reforms that gave hope for the betterment of the people, which came at an exceedingly high cost. They did away with the value of life and declared that if people would not change with the system, then it would be better that they do not exist. Therefore, it is appropriate to say that war and violence were the hallmarks of their ideology. Moreover, the only reason for doing all of that was to make their countries stand eye to eye with the Western powers. Sadly, with it came unimaginable sorrow and downfall, which saw the people take their own lives, while the country hit the ground hard.

The Democratic Socialists of America

The Democratic Socialists of America saw a significant increase in their membership when Bernie Sanders and Alexandria Ocasio-Cortez took the stage to voice their support for socialism. When they began to campaign, many students heard a familiar word that had lost its meaning in the country's history – socialism. They were so carried away by all the free stuff being promised by this failed ideology that many of them embraced the idea. They failed to realize that all those promises are unrealistic, as the country's total GDP cannot pay for them. The same old tricks socialists and communists have used to deceive their people. As the saying goes, they who do not learn history are doomed to repeat it.

Even some older Americans seem to be buying into the garbage. We are, as of now, encountering many Americans question whether they should redo the political and financial frameworks through and through, or not. However, this did not happen before. Nearly 50 years ago, the New Left raised some issues about capitalism, racism, imperialism, sexism, and many others that should be resolved. Toward the end of the 1960s, the New Communist Movement was vocal about these issues. The New Communist Movement was a collection of factions in the Marxist-Leninist ideologues. They believed in creating a society that will be governed by Marxism and Leninism. Democratic Socialists of America is an entirely different story. Its end game is a communist, Godless society, and every professing Christian must be aware of this danger. You don't need to hold fast to a specific belief system in order to be a member of the Democratic Socialist Party of America. One belief of the New Communist Movement is that there are grave threats in associations based on a belief system. They direct an association toward ideological purism, making everything to rely on an ideological convention, giving an undue position to the top administration, which probably has aced that belief system.

Regardless of these founding points, capitalism became the best system that the world is witnessing today. There have been many cases where there was an unending debate about why Donald Trump is still favored after all the hatred. Donald Trump, in this case, easily wins over Bernie Sanders because of the latter's ability to unpack the deceptions of the socialists. On the other hand, Donald Trump is sticking to a system that caters only to the situations necessary for humans to succeed, which are identified only through the concepts of individual rights. The United States came closest to a capitalistic system in the late 19th century. Since then, there has been a huge increase in the control of property by the state. Today's system in the state is not entirely capitalism, but it is getting there through the vision of Donald Trump.

Chapter 9
The King Who Serves

The only way that you can make a person trust you to provide them with happiness is through service. The moment someone benefits from something another person did, it does not take long for him or her to be a supporter. That is how the world wants to work these days. The politicians become shepherds to the flock of people that are looking for guidance, and they manage to do that by providing them with the best service.

Just like the main theme of this book, I want to bring one system to your attention whose service raises no questions. In the list of the most influential men, Ludwig von Mises is as important as Karl Marx is. Ludwig von Mises is the one that brought about the change in the economic system that I, like a million others, think to be the best in today's era.

Ludwig von Mises is known as one of the most influential Austrian economists of his era. He was a promoter of laissez-faire economics and a faithful opponent of all shades of socialism and interventionism. Ludwig von Mises also wrote comprehensively on fiscal economics and inflation. Mises not only taught at the University of Vienna and New York University but also published his most popular work in 1949, entitled Human Action. Ludwig von Mises was born in 1881 in Austria-Hungary. His parents, who were Jewish, were part of the Austro-Hungarian upper class, as well as a distant relative to a second-in-command of the Liberal Party to the Austrian Parliament.

Ludwig von Mises displayed academic gifts early on in his life through the flawless use of Polish, French, German, and Latin. Under the influence of a writer named Carl Menger, one of the founders of the Austrian School of Economics, Mises began his study of politics. To this day, Carl Menger is highly respected for developing the subjective side of economics. This development in the subject meant that all the contributors in a trade exchange achieved significance and that there are no losers in it.

Ludwig von Mises graduated in law with a Juris doctorate and commenced his career as a civil servant in 1906. However, before graduating, he was already under the influence of Eugen von Böhm-Bawerk, another Austrian economist. Although he was hired for a trainee position in a law firm, Ludwig von Mises never forgot his interest in economics. As time passed, he started lecturing on the topic and eventually became a member of the Vienna Chamber of Commerce and Industry. His duties did not end there because he served as an economist to the War Department of Austria and in World War I as a front officer.

Through the association with the Vienna Chamber of Commerce and Industry, von Mises saw that he was not the only one interested in economics and the result of human behavior. As he progressed through the ranks, Ludwig von Mises became a chief economist and an economic adviser to Engelbert Dollfuss, an Austrian Chancellor who strongly believed in an Austrian dictatorship but was also against the Nazis.

His influence on the implementation and effects of the system made Ludwig von Mises a respectable figure in the United States of America as well. There is a libertarian academic organization known as the Ludwig von Mises Institute, named in his honor. It celebrates and extends his teachings and writings of the study of human behavior in regard to economics. Through this, Ludwig von Mises began to strengthen his argument that capitalism is the king who served, not ruled. There was a constant battle between the ideologies that Karl Marx brought to establish a system that he believed could not be countered. With the countries adapting socialism and slowly inviting their doomsday to hit them harder than expected, Ludwig von Mises saw the issue that needed to be addressed. That is when he delivered nine lectures that have been entitled, Marxism Unmasked in 1952. These lectures were delivered from June 23 to July 3 at the San Francisco Public Library, which was sponsored by The Freeman magazine.

It all started when writers began to write about the problems that Marx brought with the system that the Western powers were implementing. The harshest critique came from Ludwig von Mises' own professor, Eugen von Böhm-Bawerk. And from there onwards, the entire momentum was picked up and elevated by his student, Mises.

During World War I and its abrupt aftermath, there was wholehearted confidence that the age of government organization had finally come. Following the Bolshevik Revolution in 1917 in Russia, Lenin's Marxist regime enforced war communism. It was an indication that it was not just a device of emergency to fight the anti-socialists during the civil war, but it was also a leap into a fully planned society. Nearly a couple of years later, at an Austrian Economic Society meeting, Ludwig von Mises delivered a paper entitled, Economic Calculation in the Socialist Commonwealth. This was published the following year in a German journal. Mises used this piece as the focal point of his article that he published two years later in 1922, which was entitled, Socialism: An Economic and Sociological Analysis.

There was continuous criticism from both ends from two of the great names in political history. When it came to capitalism, Marx accepted that capitalism contributed to the huge development of the economy's modern beneficial ability. However, as he would strongly think, it made two-region social classes: the bourgeoisie and the proletariat. The bourgeoisie was portrayed as the ones that controlled production and the workers. The working class was portrayed as an incredible inverse since the workers who claimed and controlled only gave the methods for production. Marx states that as the bourgeoisie had control to an ever-increasing extent, they will influence the dehumanization of the working class and strip them of all that they claim. When the low class has been pushed to their limit, they will ascend and oust the bourgeoisie, as they will have the numbers on their side. The lower class will at that point control all methods for production and work, and they will bring freedom to the condition of capitalism and thus, supplant it with socialism, a financial framework opposite to capitalism where the common laborers, or the lower class, will control the methods for creation.

Von Mises had an incredible inverse view on capitalism as compared to Marx. Nowadays, he is referred to as a protector of capitalism, which is as it should be. He accepted that capitalism was "not just large-scale manufacturing, but rather it was large scale manufacturing to fulfill the necessities of the majority." These two giants, one a solid devotee to communist reasoning, Marx, and the other a solid adherent to industrialist thinking, Von Mises, can be truly considered to comprehend the possibility of capitalism in general and how it will influence society. Mises was ahead of his time in his examination of the manners by which capitalism and liberalism had changed marriage and the family.

Mises started his resolution by trusting socialists with their ideology. He accepted that communism would substitute conscious planning for the "anarchy of production" of the commercial center, the term utilized by Karl Marx. It implies that instead of depending on costs and benefits to reveal what we should create and how we should deliver it, socialism would nullify private property, trade, markets, costs, benefits, and substitute collective ownership and basic leadership to address those inquiries. Under capitalism, we permit private proprietors of the methods for production to try different things with options and later identify the ideal ones.

Ludwig von Mises put an interesting question forward in his 1920 published article. He asked whether it was possible to identify what people want and how to produce it without any markets and private property involved in the means of production. While there may be various technologically plausible methods for producing a particular good, just one of those ways utilizes the least important assets conceivable, and it is, in this manner, the most financially effective approach. The test of economic calculation is having a procedure for making sense of which of the innovatively doable choices is the least inefficient one. For the public to address that question, it must have a few methods of comparison. Mises offers an assortment of reasons why utilizing a portion of work time and incorporating the distinctions in the quality of labor, as the Marxists recommended, will not work. What should be resolved is how a lot of elective data sources are valued, and after the marginal transformation of the economic theory, the same is regarded as financial incentives dependent on the subjective valuations of individual choosers. So, the best way to access and sum up those valuations in a structure, which takes into consideration the comparisons among alternatives, is that solitary market costs can perform that role efficiently.

"In any social order, even under Socialism, it can very easily be decided which kind and what number of consumption goods should be produced. No one has ever denied that. But once this decision has been made, there still remains the problem of ascertaining how the existing means of production can be used most effectively to produce these goods in question. In order to solve this problem it is necessary that there should be economic calculation. And economic calculation can only take place by means of money

prices established in the market for production goods in a society resting on private property in the means of production. That is to say, there must exist money prices of land, raw materials, semi-manufactures; that is to say, there must be money wages and interest rates."

To have market prices, the general public needs to have markets. In addition, markets require individuals to participate in exchanging goods and services, as summarized above. One can't trade what one doesn't own, and Mises contends that on the off chance that normal financial estimation requires costs that mirror people's valuations, responsibility for creation methods must be private.

As with private property in the production methods, capital products have certifiable market costs that mirror the valuations of proprietors and shoppers. Those costs are essential for deciding how best to deliver what individuals need. Hence, private property in the methods of production is important for addressing the subject of economic calculation. The biggest argument between socialism and capitalism is the fact that healthcare becomes the deciding issue. Proclaiming that government-provided healthcare should be a privilege does not answer the questions about what the government should deliver and how it will realize how to create something while keeping everything else balanced. All choices about production require the ability to take part in economic calculation, and that requires costs, benefits, and private property. Without market costs, producers are simply groping in darkness. With minor variations, this exercise applies to all propositions to substitute government proprietorship and make strategic arrangements for the market.

The problem with democratic socialism is that democratic or not, it is still socialism, according to Ludwig von Mises. He comprehensively explains the long transformative procedures that created the liberal order as an order from violence to an agreement as the premise of social collaboration. Mises objects to the fact that, in the economic realm, the standard of law and the advancement of property rights and agreement defeated the utilization of violence as the prevalent method for deciding and evolving ownership.

The rise of market foundations was a push away from violence toward a contract. In the political realm, the improvement of vote-based procedures and foundations offered a peaceful method of political transition as opposed to the viciousness experienced in governments of pre-democratic structures. For Mises, the great advantage of democracy is the peaceful transfer of power in accordance with the agreement-like guidelines of a liberal constitutional order.

As a way of highlighting the disadvantages of socialism, Ludwig von Mises addresses the issue of marriage. He compares the nature of marriage in "the age of violence" to the marriage in "the age of contract."

"The characteristic of love, the overvaluing of the object, cannot exist when women occupy the position of contempt which they occupy under the principle of violence. For under this system, she is merely a slave, but it is the nature of love to conceive her as a queen."

Where marriage was an imposition of male power and where women were basically the property of the men they wedded, marriage was a relationship described by both disparity and hopelessness, particularly for women. Mises contends that the love and parts of marriage that we underestimate in the time of agreement were impractical during the time of savagery. Sentimental love and marriage were, to a great extent, diverse during this period. Love-based marriage could become a reality only when marriage requires consent and agreement between two equal individuals. For Mises, society thrives best on human participation. Therefore, collaboration can only be created when people see the benefits they will have from their efforts and the development of trade that results from it. The differences in human abilities and talents are important reasons for the division of labor and the differences in wages. A more productive worker receives a higher wage than a less productive one. This is what drives competition, innovation, and industry in a capitalist system.

Trade makes the obligations of peaceful relationships that start the change from the period of violence to the time of the agreement. This procedure is a "unifying influence" for Mises. It essentially clarifies how the liberal order emerged and will keep on making progress if we enable liberal foundations to carry out their responsibility. The basic idea of capitalism is social harmony through the quest for personal responsibility. Under capitalism, an individual's quest for his very own financial self-interest benefits the economic self-interest of others. By enabling every person to act unrestricted by government regulations, capitalism allows wealth to be made in the most proficient way conceivable, which, at last, increases life expectancy, expands the economic odds, and makes accessible a consistently developing supply of products for every individual.

The free market works in such a manner that as one person creates more wealth for himself, he simultaneously opens the door for every other person with the same opportunity as well. This implies that as the rich become richer, the financial position of the poor also improves. It must be understood that capitalism serves the economic interests of all classes, including the proletarians.

Despite generally held convictions, capitalism is not a framework that favors only the wealthy. Amusingly, socialism leads to the systematic abuse of labor. Since the socialist state holds an all-inclusive imposing business model on labor and production, no financial motivation exists in the socialist state other than minimum physical subsistence for the laborers. While capitalism has been there just as long as socialism has, the question that is on everyone's minds is, *"Can it still work?"*

The Industrial Revolution was the key event in the rise and shift from capitalism as it targeted the industry as a whole. After the French Revolution and the Napoleonic Wars had dismantled the remaining bastions of feudalism, Adam Smith's arrangements were progressively explored. The arrangements of 19th-century political liberalism included unhindered commerce, sound money, adjusted spending plans, and less relief for the poor. The development of modern capitalism and the improvement of the production line framework in the 19th century also made a massive new class of mechanical laborers whose hopeless conditions, for the most part, propelled the progressive way of thinking of Karl Marx, which was shortsighted.

In the decades following World War II, the economies of the significant capitalist nations, all of which had adopted some form of the welfare state, performed well. They reestablished a portion of the trust in the industrialist framework that had been lost during the 1930s. While there is no doubt that each system had its bad times and questionable phases, capitalism needs to be remembered as the flourishing point of every country. Over the previous century, the total population grew by 4%, the world economy expanded by 14%, and the worldwide per capita pay significantly increased. In that time, positive future forecasts increased by about 66% due to noticeable progress in medical care coverage, improved nutrition, and different comforts afforded by the market economy. Private enterprise is, truth be told, very flexible to address the issues of society as they arise. After some time, a guideline was developed to address the rising issues, for example, restraining infrastructure control, intrigue, price control, and a variety of job-killing regulations. One major problem is reacting to environmental change.

There are questions about the theories and models that are used to analyze, clarify, and set strategies for the market. Two of them that have received notable consideration are neoclassical economics aspects and principal-agent theories. The two theories act as the foundation for the establishment of the broad training and practice, as they are based on outrageous and rather terrible rearrangements of people driven by greed, materialism, and irresponsibility. The type of capitalism we have today has developed over hundreds of years to meet emerging needs, but additionally, it has been molded and twisted by private interests. In recent times, the political economy has been defiled most prominently by "a developing plot among government and giant corporations." This issue has turned out to be the one that has had a significant impact after the money-related emergency and the bombed strategies that proved to be successful. The answers to these issues are both policy arrangements and partnerships to advocate for them.

At the end of the day, the answers for environmental change must originate from the market and, more specifically, from businesses. The market is the most dominant foundation on earth, and business is the most dominant factor inside it. Business makes the merchandise and ventures that we depend upon, such as the clothes we wear, the food we eat, the types of devices we use, and the infrastructures we live and work in.

Organizations can rise above national limits when they have assets that surpass that of numerous nations. On the flip side, if businesses don't provide answers to a carbon-neutral world, there will be no solutions.

It can be said that capitalism can develop to the point that it can address our present climate emergency. However, this cannot take place by either dismantling the foundations that are currently existing nor by depending on the consideration of a free enterprise market. This will, ultimately, require keen pioneers to create an insightfully organized market.

Chapter 10
Populism – An Ideology to Regain Lost Glory

Populism is now on the rise with the election of Donald Trump as the President of the United States. Furthermore, there are a few countries in Europe where the right-wing populism strongly opposes uncontrolled immigration. In politics, the term populism can have different meanings depending on who is using it and what their political goals are. At its root, populism is a belief in the power of regular people, and in their right to have control over their government rather than a small group of political insiders or a wealthy elite.

The word populism comes from the Latin word for "people," populus. Populism's ideology considers a society to be divided into two camps, known as the corrupt elite and the pure people. It further believes that politics should be based on the will of the citizens. Populism combines the ideologies of liberalism, socialism, and nationalism in its philosophy. Thus, it is safe to say that it merges the left and right political spectrum, which further branches out to left-wing populism and right-wing populism. This type of ideology contains a person who labels himself or herself to be the "voice of the people," much like the U.S. president.

"We assembled here today are issuing a new decree to be heard in every city, in every foreign capital, and in every hall of power. From this day forward, a new vision will govern our land. From this moment on, it's going to be America First. Every decision on trade, on taxes, on immigration, on foreign affairs, will be made to benefit American workers and American families. We must protect our borders from the ravages of other countries making our products, stealing our companies, and destroying our jobs. Protection will lead to great prosperity and strength. I will fight for you with every breath in my body – and I will never, ever let you down. America will start winning again, winning like never before. We will bring back our jobs. We will bring back our borders. We will bring back our wealth. And we will bring back our dreams. We will build new roads, and highways, and bridges, and airports, and tunnels, and railways all across our wonderful nation. We will get our people off of welfare and back to work – rebuilding our country with American

hands and American labor. We will follow two simple rules: Buy American and Hire American. We will seek friendship and goodwill with the nations of the world – but we do so with the understanding that it is the right of all nations to put their own interests first. We do not seek to impose our way of life on anyone, but rather to let it shine as an example for everyone to follow. We will reinforce old alliances and form new ones – and unite the civilized world against Radical Islamic Terrorism, which we will eradicate completely from the face of the Earth. At the bedrock of our politics will be a total allegiance to the United States of America, and through our loyalty to our country, we will rediscover our loyalty to each other. When you open your heart to patriotism, there is no room for prejudice. The Bible tells us, "how good and pleasant it is when God's people live together in unity.

We must speak our minds openly, debate our disagreements honestly, but always pursue solidarity. When America is united, America is totally unstoppable. There should be no fear – we are protected, and we will always be protected. We will be protected by the great men and women of our military and law enforcement and, most importantly, we are protected by God. Finally, we must think big and dream even bigger. In America, we understand that a nation is only living as long as it is striving. We will no longer accept politicians who are all talk and no action – constantly complaining but never doing anything about it. The time for empty talk is over. Now arrives the hour of action. Do not let anyone tell you it cannot be done. No challenge can match the heart and fight and spirit of America. We will not fail. Our country will thrive and prosper again. We stand at the birth of a new millennium, ready to unlock the mysteries of space, to free the Earth from the miseries of disease, and to harness the energies, industries and technologies of tomorrow. A new national pride will stir our souls, lift our sights, and heal our divisions. It is time to remember that old wisdom our soldiers will never forget: that whether we are black or brown or white, we all bleed the same red blood of patriots, we all enjoy the same glorious freedoms, and we all salute the same great American Flag. And whether a child is born in the urban sprawl of Detroit or the windswept plains of Nebraska, they look up at the same night sky, they fill their heart with the same dreams, and they are infused with the breath of life by the same almighty Creator.

So to all Americans, in every city near and far, small and large, from mountain to mountain, and from ocean to ocean, hear these words:

You will never be ignored again. Your voice, your hopes, and your dreams, will define our American destiny. And your courage and goodness and love will forever guide us along the way. Together, We Will Make America Strong Again. We Will Make America Wealthy Again. We Will Make America Proud Again. We Will Make America Safe Again.

And, Yes, Together, We Will Make America Great Again. Thank you, God Bless You, And God Bless America."

–Donald Trump

These compelling and convincing words came straight out of Donald Trump's mouth during his inaugural address in Washington, D.C., on January 20, 2017, after taking the oath to become the United States' 45th president. This speech was to let the people of America know that they are looking at a bright future under the rule of a person who has a populist vision, which was also America's first. Furthermore, by describing Americans as people who are generally similar and share similar opportunities, Trump plays into the possibility that racism will never be an issue in American life again. Any individual who opposes this vision and hope is merely playing the role of a victim.

Nevertheless, the words mentioned above caught the attention of millions that listened to him that day. Donald Trump undoubtedly believes in his vision for America, and all can already see the results that are coming in, such as the economy, which has reached an unmatchable high, better than ever. Since Donald Trump heavily emphasizes the fact that he is a populist, we first need to learn what that term means.

A pure populist leader, like Donald Trump, professes to speak only for the people and the will of the people. They will use terms such as taxpaying and ordinary people to refer to the people and put their interests above anything else. The left-wing and right-wing populists oppose the power of the big corporations and wealth that suppresses the common man. In short, they will do anything to fight against individuals or corporations that are not benefitting the people of the country, thereby confronting elite liberals. As years have passed, the term "we the people" is becoming clearer. It is understood that this term means all the citizens of the nation, regardless of race, color, customs, the time they have spent as citizens, and religion. According to the structure that this ideology brings, it tries to protect the interest of the people and amplify it through a democratic change instead of a riot against the elite.

In the United States, the term was applied to the Populist Movement program in 1892, which led to the rise of Populist or People's Party. A considerable number of the group's or party's requests were later embraced as laws or constitutional amendments. The populist demand for a direct democratic government rule through mainstream initiatives and choices also became a reality in various states in America.

Populism is frequently connected with an authoritarian type of legislative system. Following this definition, a populist legislative system centers around an inspiring leader who has won the people's support in the highest number of states.

In the 20th Century, populism came to be related to the political style and program of Latin American pioneers like Juan Perón, Hugo Chávez, and Getúlio Vargas. Populism was usually understood as a criticism of a leader for giving into the people's fear and energy. Depending on one's perspective on populism, a populist program can, in this manner, mean an ideology that advances the interests of regular citizens and the nation in general, or an ideology that tries to redistribute the wealth of the nation. This is done regardless of the consequences for the nation, like debt or inflation.

The populist society existed just as long as the previous systems that the world knows about. Its first movement began in 1849 and lasted until 1860. They were known as the Know-Nothings. The Know-Nothings utilized the principles of white Christian's matchless quality to hold onto political control over the minority instead of workers and Catholics.

The Know-Nothings came out of a mysterious Protestant society known as the Order of the Star-Spangled Banner, where urban packs pestered foreigners and spread purposeful political publicity against them. From that point forward, they formed into a third ideological group and exploited vulnerable sides of the Whigs and the Democrats. The Know-Nothings authoritatively embraced the name "the American Party" in 1854 and took hold of the Massachusetts Council. In the end, when its individuals did not create any approach tending to slavery trends, and when most of their individuals had escaped to join the Republicans by 1860, they lost support. Then came the Greenback Party that lasted for ten years from 1874 to 1884. They were a bunch of farming communities that originated through the Granges vicinity. The Greenbacks needed to start inflation to help with the debts and encouraged an eight-hour workday as a piece of a more extensive productive activity, in order to achieve more economic gain. They ran as presidential candidates through 1884 before disbanding in the end.

The populist system then found an appropriate name with the Populist Party in 1892. They had adopted a lot of the Greenback Party's agenda by supporting an instant restriction on remote land proprietorship, state control of the railways, and truncated workdays. The women were highly involved in the Party as they organized meetings, spoke at rallies, and wrote articles about the group in editorial pieces.

However, with the influence of black people, the group made sure to stress the support for white people alone. In 1894, their support was slowly weakening, and by the year 1908, the party was dissolved. When the group's ruling power came to an end, it was time for someone to take charge on his own. That person was William Jennings Bryan. The self-announced protector of the common man and average workers, William Jennings Bryan, was chosen for Congress in Nebraska in 1890 as a Democrat, and later won more support through his factual speeches. In 1896 at the Democratic show, an aggressive speech against the gold standard and supporting the silver currency to help diminish farm debt was acclaimed to the point that he was nominated to become the President. Unfortunately, he lost that political election but replicated the same experience on more than a couple of occasions. After his involvement in the Spanish Civil War, he was known as an anti-imperialist.

He was also an enemy of imposing business models and wrote a paper entitled 'The Commoner,' which established him as a revolutionary populist. Bryan became the secretary of state in 1912 but resigned over a disagreement over the European War, which would become known as World War I in the end. He upheld a neutral position and committed his remaining time to women's suffrage, which is women's right to vote in elections and **pushing for Prevention, an important time for law during the Civil War**. Another renowned figure in the populist movement was Huey Long, who led the impactful movement from 1918 to 1935, which was the first of the 20th Century as well. He had a large wave of supporters because he supported the anti-corporate efforts, which he observed during his time in the Louisiana Railroad Commission until becoming a governor from 1918 to 1928.

He gave the police more power, introduced associates into government offices, and gained power from the government. He financed education, architecture, and energy programs by implementing taxes on the rich. In 1930, Long became a U.S. senator but maintained his power inside Louisiana through a Secretive Governor. By keeping an eye on the administration, Long began the 'Share the Wealth Club' that offered a rigorous plan to redistribute wealth.

Fast-forwarding to the late-90s, the era saw some moderate conservationist populism with the presidential crusades of Ross Perot. Ross Perot won 18.9% of the vote in 1992 and 8.4% in 1996. Television and radio media additionally observed a rise in populist Conservative people like Rush Limbaugh and Fox News' hosts, with Matt Drudge and Andrew Breitbart on the Internet, and authors like Ann Coulter. Populism had a significant impact during the 2000s. The Tea Party was a moderate development that showed up in 2009 after the appointment of President Barack Obama. The Tea Party rode a rush of notions about Obama to push the Republican Party further to the point of Libertarianism. It additionally became related to the Freedom Caucus, which was another populist Conservative development.

Occupy Wall Street, the populist movement of the mid-2000s, grew following the fiscal emergency of 2011. The leader-less development focused on looking for monetary change and prosecution of the enormous banks behind the money-related crisis. Its members organized great marches and established semi-lasting camps for protests in cities. Despite the fact that it was a dynamic movement to a great extent and was noted for the inclusion of revolutionary groups, its anti-bank and anti-corporate attitude also pulled in some right-wingers, libertarians, and others for support.

When we look at the current era in Donald Trump's reign, his populist movement has already wrapped up more than a few accomplishments. President Trump entered the Oval Office as a populist contrary to the predictions of leftish pundits and the Democrats. In any case, after a year, the traditionalist Heritage Foundation, whose strategy is to assemble and spread conservative policies of the public, presently proclaims that Trump has a more favorable rating than Ronald Reagan, who also used the Foundation. Trump embraced around 64% of the Heritage incentive. This implies that the organization reordered 334 of the research organization's one of a kind strategy proposal. By comparison, Reagan embraced only 49% of the Heritage incentive, thereby making 2017 a profound year for Heritage. The Heritage greeted Trump wholeheartedly. He required a detailed blueprint, and they had a store of strategy propositions that were good to go. Thus, without his own opinions, the ideological 'trump card' of an executive embraced the thoughts of the greatest conservative research organization in Washington.

The way that Trump has taken up their plans talks a lot about their impact. Moreover, the way that Heritage mentions Trump in a similar breath as Reagan mirrors the condition of present-day practical conservatism. Putting aside the fact that understanding the cutoff points of government is essential to our constitutional republic, the right-wingers appear to treat conservatism as a restriction. They do not mind that Reagan had the option to speak in the same circumstances, while simultaneously being successful in passing the policies. What is required now, according to the final study of the conservative consensus, is somebody ready to tear down the authoritative state's status quo. Thus, it is safe to say that Heritage has discovered that requirement in Donald Trump.

Trump is in his fourth year in office, and the unprecedented accomplishments are astounding. It is becoming clearer that this man, who had no political experience as compared to the people he defeated, is taking the western nations in the right direction.

The List Of President Trump's Accomplishments So Far Trump Administration Accomplishments January 2020

January 14, 2020

Below is a summary of the top accomplishments achieved under President Trump's administration.

Economy

President Trump's policies have put the American economy into high gear.

- Since President Trump was elected, 7.3 million jobs have been created.

- In 2019, 2.1 new jobs were created.

- In 2019, 1.5 million jobs were added for women. This accounts for more than 50% of total job gains for the first time ever.

- Over 500,000 manufacturing jobs have been created since the President was elected.

- The current unemployment rate is 3.5%, a 50-year low.

- Highlights of December's jobs report:

- 174,000 jobs were created in December.

- December marked the 22nd consecutive month that the unemployment rate has been at or below 4%.

- For 22 consecutive months, wage growth has been near or above 3%.

- Throughout the Trump Administration, we have seen record low unemployment for women, African Americans, Latino Americans, and Asian Americans. In December:

- African American unemployment rate was at 5.9%.

- The Hispanic American unemployment rate remained at a near-record low of 4.2%.

- The Asian American unemployment rate was 2.5%, near a historic low.

- The adult women's unemployment rate hit 3.2%, the lowest since 1953.

- The Dow Jones Industrial Average hit record highs over 100 times under President Trump.

- Under President Trump, 7 million people have come off food stamps.

- Under President Trump's leadership, Congress passed historic tax cuts and relief for hardworking Americans. The Tax Cuts and Jobs Act is the first major tax reform signed in 30 years.

- As a result of the historic tax cuts, nearly 9,000 Opportunity Zones were created in all 50 states, D.C., and five territories. Opportunity Zones will spur $100 billion in private capital investment and impact nearly 35 million Americans.

- The Tax Cuts and Jobs Act increased the Child Tax Credit by 100%, keeping more money in the pockets of hardworking mothers.

- Economic confidence rebounded to record highs under President Trump because his pro-growth policies have and continue to put American workers and businesses first.

- President Trump has rolled back unnecessary job-killing regulations at a historic pace.

- The Administration has cut eight and a half regulations for every new rule.

- This far exceeds the promise made to cut two regulations for every one regulation added.

- Regulatory costs have been slashed by nearly $50 billion and have saved taxpayers $220 billion once actions are implemented.

- The deregulation efforts will save American households an estimated $3,100 per year.

- The Administration formed the Governors' Initiative on Regulatory Innovation, which aims to better align State and Federal efforts to cut additional unnecessary regulations and costs.

Immigration

President Trump is working to secure our border.

- President Trump is fulfilling his promise to build a border wall, with sizable portions already finished or under construction.

- It's expected that 450 miles will be finished by the end of 2020.

- The Trump Administration has constructed 100 miles of the new border wall system.

- Currently, 167 miles of wall is under construction in high entry sectors such as San Diego, El Centro, El Paso, and Yuma.

- The new wall has contributed to a 56% overall decrease in the number of illegal migrant arrivals at the border.

- Under President Trump, the U.S. Border Patrol has arrested hundreds of members of dangerous gangs.

- The President has strongly enforced our nation's immigration laws by cracking down on illegal immigration and taking aim at "sanctuary cities."

- President Trump has called on Congress to close dangerous loopholes such as "Catch and Release," end chain migration, and end the visa lottery program, which enables illegal immigration.

- The Administration is looking to close the Flores Settlement Agreement that requires the government to release families into the country after 20 days. This loophole has been exploited by smugglers who use children as pawns to enter our country.

- We are closing asylum loopholes – recently, the Administration instituted a new rule requiring migrants who come to our border to have previously applied and been denied to a country they passed through.

- The Trump Administration announced they are releasing a "Public Charge Rule" that will ensure non-citizens do not abuse our nation's public benefits. This rule will go into effect on 10/15/19.

- President Trump was successful in his efforts to get Mexico and the Northern Triangle countries to step up and help stop the crisis at the border.

- President Trump's successful negotiations have led to a 28% drop in migrants taken into custody in June.

- In May, President Trump announced a new immigration proposal that would modernize our system and secure the border.

- The Administration has made it a priority to end human trafficking and is using many resources to do so.

- The Administration provided funding to support the National Human Trafficking Hotline.

- The Anti-Trafficking Coordination Team (ACTeam) initiative more than doubled convictions of human traffickers and increased the number of defendants charged in ACTeam districts.

Foreign Policy

President Trump has restored our nation's standing in the world and is standing up to bad actors.

- The United States has successfully decimated ISIS.

- Under President Trump, the number one terrorist leader Abu Bakr al-Baghdadi was taken out.

- President Trump ordered the killing of Qassem Soleimani, the head of Iran's elite Quds Force and an evil, ruthless, and deadly terrorist.

- President Trump fulfilled his promise to recognize Jerusalem Israel's capital city and moved the U.S. Embassy.

- President Trump held two historic summits with North Korean leader Kim Jong Un, further demonstrating the Administration's commitment to a denuclearized Korean peninsula.

- President Trump withdrew the U.S. from the Iran Nuclear Agreement and instituted the toughest sanctions in history to drive the regime's oil exports to zero.

- In June 2019, President Trump signed an executive order that authorizes expanded sanctions against Iran.

- The Administration has vigorously and quickly enforced red lines against regimes and individuals that use chemical weapons.

- The Trump Administration has imposed sanctions on Russian entities and individuals previously indicted for their roles in Russian interference in our election.

- The Trump Administration imposed hard-hitting sanctions against Iran's national bank.

Trade

President Trump is delivering on his promise to correct trade imbalances.

- The Trump Administration had taken unprecedented steps to modernize and improve trading practices and negotiate freer, fairer, and reciprocal trade agreements with our global allies.

- President Trump has kept his promise to deliver a modern and rebalanced trade deal to replace NAFTA. The United States – Mexico – Canada Agreement (U.S.M.C.A.)

- The U.S.C.M.A. will spur economic growth, create 176,000 jobs, add $68.2 billion to the U.S. economy, and raise wages.

- President Trump negotiated a new United States-Japan trade deal with Prime Minister Shinzo Abe. Japan is one of our strongest economic partners, and this trade deal builds on that partnership. It is a big win for American farmers, ranchers, workers, and businesses.

- The Administration revised the United States -Korea Free Trade Agreement (KORUS) to make it more beneficial to American workers.

- The President and European Union President Juncker agreed to a new trade deal that strengthens and reforms our trade relationship. The agreement:

- Works toward zero tariffs, zero non-tariff barriers, zero subsidies on non-automotive industrial goods.

- Makes it easier for the E.U. to purchase liquefied gas.

- Reduces trade and bureaucratic obstacles between the U.S. and the E.U.

- Addresses unfair trade practices.

- President Trump agreed to a phase one trade deal with China that includes a strong enforcement mechanism.

- President Trump withdrew the United States from the flawed Trans-Pacific Partnership.

- President Trump has forced our allies to recommit to NATO.

- The Trump Administration has protected farmers from unfair trade practices by authorizing $12 billion in aid to the American agricultural heartland under The Commodity Credit Corporation Charter Act.

Judicial

President Trump continues to reshape the Federal judiciary at a record pace and is following through on his promise to appoint judges who will uphold the Constitution and the rule of law.

- President Trump continues to reshape the Federal judiciary at a record pace.

- President Trump has installed more Federal court judges than any president in the past four decades.

- The President is following through on his promise to appoint judges who will uphold the Constitution and the rule of law for generations to come.

- President Trump has nominated, and the Senate has confirmed a grand total of 187 Article III judges.

- 2 Supreme Court Justices – Justice Gorsuch and Justice Kavanaugh.

- 50 Circuit Court judges.

- 133 District Court judges.

- 2 Court of International Trade Judges

- President Trump's judicial confirmations have "flipped" 3 – 2nd, 3rd, 11th Circuits – Federal appeals courts to Republican.

- In 2018, President Trump broke the record for the most circuit court of appeals judges (29) confirmed in the first two years of a presidency.

Health Care

President Trump has reduced the cost of health care and taken significant steps to fight the opioid epidemic.

- President Trump has prioritized fixing our broken health care system and worked with Congress to implement a system that works for all Americans.

- The President has made it clear patients with preexisting conditions will be protected.

- The individual mandate penalty has been eliminated.

- Association Health Plans have been expanded.

- Short-term, limited-duration insurance plans have been extended.

- President Trump is working to implement his plan to lower prescription drugs.

- Under the Trump Administration, we have seen the first-ever decline of average benchmark premiums on the federal health care exchange.

- The President signed an Executive Order to improve seniors' health care and improve the fiscal sustainability of Medicare.

- Reforms to expand Medicare Advantage options and Health Reimbursement Accounts have been expanded.

- President Trump mobilized his entire Administration to address the drug addiction and opioid abuse by declaring a Nationwide Public Health Emergency.

- President Trump signed the SUPPORT for Patients and Communities Act to fight the opioid epidemic.

- The Administration launched FindTreatment.gov, a public resource to help combat substance abuse.

- President Trump signed an Executive Order that increases price and quality transparency.

- The Administration has committed to ending surprise billing.

- H.H.S. is finalizing a rule that will require hospitals to make prices publicly available online and in a more consumer-friendly format.

- The Administration has proposed a rule to require insurance companies and group health plans to provide enrollees with cost estimates.

- The Trump Administration has promoted innovation and solutions to expand treatment options for Americans living with the disease, including

HIV/AIDS, kidney disease, pediatric cancer, Alzheimer's, and more.

- The Administration launched a program to provide the H.I.V. prevention drug PrEP to uninsured patients for free.

- Signed the bipartisan Tobacco-Free Youth Act to raise the nationwide age for purchasing tobacco and vaping products to 21 years old.

- Costly Obamacare taxes were repealed, including the "Cadillac tax" and the Medical Device Tax.

Environment

President Trump is promoting a clean and healthy environment for all Americans.

- The President and the Administration are continuing to pursue policies that encourage environmental protection while promoting economic growth.

- Since 2005, our energy-related carbon emissions have declined more than any other country. This is expected to decrease in 2019 and 2020.

- Our nation's environmental record is one of the strongest in the world.

- According to the White House, from 1970 to 2018, the combined emissions of the most common air pollutants fell 74% while the economy grew over 275%.

- We have the cleanest air on record and remain a global leader for access to clean drinking water. The President has taken important steps to restore, preserve, and protect our land, air, and waters.

- The Save Our Seas Act was signed into law in 2018. This law reauthorized the NOAA Marine Debris Program, promoting international action to reduce marine debris and authorizing cleanup and response actions that may be needed.

- The E.P.A. has taken significant steps to clean up our contaminated sites and hazardous sites.

- In FY2018, the E.P.A. completed cleanup work on 22 Superfund sites from the National Priorities List. This is the largest number in one year since 2005.

- The E.P.A. is more efficiently implementing air quality standards that will better protect the environment and human health.

- The President's management of our nation's lands promotes conservation while encouraging good stewardship and expanding recreational opportunities.

- Just this year, President Trump signed legislation designating 1.3 million new acres of wilderness – the largest public lands legislation in a decade.

- The Department of the Interior proposed to open more than 1 million acres of land for expanded hunting and fishing access. The President took important action to improve the management of forests to help prevent devastating forest fires.

- President Trump issued changes to the National Environmental Policy Act (N.E.P.A.) to reduce regulation and allow for infrastructure and transportation projects to move forward.

Energy

President Trump's policies have begun to unleash our nation's energy potential.

- President Trump signed an Executive Order to expand offshore oil and gas drilling and open more leases to develop offshore drilling.

- The Administration acted aggressively to increase exports of energy resources to the global market and allowed financing for coal and fossil energy projects.• President Trump has approved the infrastructure and provided the resources needed to unleash oil and gas production in the U.S.

- The Keystone XL and Dakota Access pipelines were approved, supporting an estimated total of 42,000 jobs and $2 billion in wages.

- The New Burgos Pipeline, a cross-border project that will export U.S. gasoline to Mexico, was approved.

- The Trump Administration reversed President Obama's moratorium on new leases for oil and gas development on Federal lands.

- The President rescinded President Obama's costly

Clean Power Plan.

- The President proposed the Affordable Clean Energy Rule to reduce greenhouse gasses, empower states, promote energy independence, and facilitate economic growth and job creation.• The Administration has rescinded many costly Obama-Era regulations, including the methane emissions rule that would cost American energy developers an estimated $530 million annually.• The President announced his intent to withdraw the U.S. from the unfair Paris Climate Accord.

Agriculture

President Trump and his Administration continue to help our farmers.

- In 2018, President Trump signed a sweeping new Farm Bill into law.

- The Farm Bill provides support and stability to our farmers, expands crop insurance, doubles how much farmers can borrow, and helps open new markets for our farmers.

- The President authorized the year-round sale of E15 gasoline, which boosted America's corn-growing communities.

- Red tape that has harmed American farmers have been rolled back.

- This includes eliminating the burdensome Obama-era Waters of the United States rule.

- The historic Tax Cuts and Jobs Act protected family farmers from the estate tax.

- Thanks to the President's historic tax cuts legislation, the effective tax rate for farmers is expected to fall from 17.2% to 13.9%.

- President Trump is standing up for America's farmers by negotiating fairer, freer, and more reciprocal trade deals that remove barriers and open markets for American farmers.

- President Trump negotiated the United States-Mexico-Canada Agreement (U.S.M.C.A.), getting a better deal for American farmers and ranchers.

- The U.S.M.C.A. will increase America's Agricultural exports by $2.2 billion.

- The U.S.M.C.A. will eliminate Canada's discriminatory programs that allow low-priced dairy products to undersell our nation's dairy producers.

- U.S.M.C.A. includes expanded market access for dairy products, eggs, and poultry.

- In a deal with the European Union, American soybean exports will be increased. o President Trump reached a new trade agreement with Japan. As a result, Japan will eliminate or reduce tariffs on approximately $7.2 billion in U.S. agricultural exports.

- President Trump continues to stand up to China and their unfair trade practices, which target our farmers.

- The Administration provided $16 billion in funds to support our farmers against unfair trade retaliation.

- The Trump Administration continues to support and expand markets for America's farmers.

- Japan's market has been opened to all American beef.

- Restrictions have been eliminated on:

- American pork exports to Argentina.

- American beef to Brazil.

- Idaho shipping potatoes to Japan.

- American poultry to South Korea.

- President Trump signed an Executive Order directing Federal agencies to streamline the agricultural biotechnology regulatory process.

- The Trump Administration is working to promote connectivity in rural American by investing in rural broadband. President Trump is working to protect our Nation's forests.

- In 2018, the President signed an Executive Order aimed at increasing responsible forest management and coordinating Federal, State, tribal, and local assets to prevent and combat wildfires.

- To preserve the health of our forests, the Agriculture Improvement Act of 2018 was signed into law.

- President Trump and his administration continue to provide necessary disaster relief to impacted areas.

Education

President Trump and his administration are putting students and families first.

- The President understands the importance of education and continues to declare the last week in January National School Choice Week.

- The President signed a historic Executive Order that promotes and protects free speech on college campuses.

- President Trump and his Administration support the Education Freedom Scholarships and Opportunity Act.

- In 2019, President Trump signed a memorandum that eliminates 100% of student loan debt for permanently disabled veterans.

- The President continues to work with the Department of Education to expand transparency and give students expanded access to vital information about

the career outcomes of the programs they enroll in.•
President Trump has made Historically Black
Colleges and Universities a priority, including
appropriating more money to H.B.C.U.s in one year
than any other president and establishing a
Presidential Board of Advisors on H.B.C.U.s.

- President Trump signed the FUTURE Act into law.
  The law permanently funds H.B.C.U.s and simplifies
  the FAFSA application.

- The President is committed to expanding and
  strengthening education in science, technology,
  engineering, and mathematic (S.T.E.M.).

- President Trump issued a presidential memorandum
  encouraging the Department of Education to
  promote S.T.E.M., especially Computer Science.

- President Trump directed more than $200 million per
  year to technology education grants for women and
  programs that encourage participation in S.T.E.M.
  careers.

- The President signed the bipartisan reauthorization
  of the Carl D. Perkins Career and Technical

Education Act. This law provides the necessary training for students and workers to succeed in the 21st Century.

- The President donated his 2017 second-quarter salary to the Department of Education. The funds were used to host a STEM-focused camp for students.

- President Trump signed the INSPIRE Act, which encourages N.A.S.A. to have more women and girls participate in S.T.E.M. and pursue careers in aerospace.

- The President signed an Executive Order to expand apprenticeships in America.

- President Trump has encouraged state and federal lawmakers to expand school choice.

- The administration lowered regulatory hurdles and restored flexibility to schools with respect to menus in their cafeterias.

- President Trump is committed to making our schools safer.

- President Trump encouraged passage of the STOP School Violence Act to provide funding grants to schools to improve security measures.

- The Administration established a Commission on School Safety to examine ways to make schools safer for all students and teachers.

- Additionally, the Administration proposed a new $5 billion annual tax credit to promote school choice. Two-thirds of black Americans support this move.

Military and Veterans

President Trump is protecting America and our allies by rebuilding our military and ensuring our veterans receive the care they deserve.

- President Trump has restored American military strength.

- Under President Trump's leadership, Congress passed three historic National Defense Authorization Acts (NDAA).

- The FY2020 NDAA includes a much needed 3.1% pay raise for our troops.

- The FY2020 NDAA establishes the United States Space Force to ensure American dominance in space.

- President Trump signed the Veterans Accountability and Whistleblower Protection Act to allow senior officials in the Department of Veterans Affairs (V.A.) to fire failing employees and establish safeguards to protect whistleblowers.

- The President signed the V.A. Choice and Quality Employment Act of 2017 to authorize $2.1 billion in additional funds for the Veterans Choice Program (V.C.P.).

- The Trump Administration created a new White House V.A. Hotline, staffed by veterans and family members.

- The Administration has secured a record of $8.6 billion in funding for mental health services to end the tragedy of veteran suicide.

- The Trump Administration has created the PREVENTS initiative, a task force aimed at unifying the efforts of government, businesses, and nonprofit groups to help our veterans.

- The President has secured $73.1 billion for the Department of Veterans Affairs – the highest funding for the V.A. in history.

- Veterans Affairs increased transparency and accountability by launching an online "Access and Quality Tool." This provides veterans a way to access wait time and quality of care data.

- In 2019, President Trump signed a memorandum that eliminates 100% of student loan debt for permanently disabled veterans.

- The President also called upon all 50 states to ensure that disabled veterans do not pay state tax on their forgiven debts.

- The unemployment rate among veterans is at a record low of 2.8%.

- 9.1 million veterans are employed.

- The number of unemployed veterans has been reduced by 40% under President Trump.

- In November 2019, President Trump became the first president to walk in the New York City Veterans Day Parade.

Women

Under President Trump's administration, women have been empowered to reach their economic potential.

- Women have experienced record low unemployment under President Trump.

- Since he was elected, President Trump has created over 4.3 million new jobs for women.

- In 2019, 1.5 million jobs were added for women. This accounts for more than 50% of total job gains for the first time ever.

- In December, the adult women's unemployment rate hit 3.2%, the lowest since 1953.

- The unemployment rate among women has been under 4% for 18 straight months.

- During the President's first year in office, the number of American women in poverty fell by nearly 600,000.

- Thanks to the Tax Cuts and Jobs Act, the child tax credit was doubled to $2,000 per child.

- President Trump was the first president to include a paid family leave policy to budget proposals.

- The FY2020 NDAA included paid parental leave for federal workers.

- The President and his Administration are committed to keeping families and communities safe.

- The Trump Administration has prioritized empowering women to pursue careers and realize their economic potential.

- President Trump directed more than $200 million per year to technology education grants for women and programs that encourage participation in S.T.E.M. careers.

- President Trump signed an Executive Order establishing the National Council For The American Worker.

- Over 300 companies and associations of all sizes and industry have signed the Administration's Pledge to

America's Workers, promising to create more than 14 million education, training, and skill-building opportunities over the next five years.

- Ivanka Trump created the Women's Global Development and Prosperity Initiative (W-GDP) to help 50 million women in 22 developing countries realize their economic potential by 2025.

- Additional Trump Administration efforts to empower women globally include:

- The Women Entrepreneurs Finance Initiative (We-Fi): Aims to mobilize more than $2.6 billion in capital for women entrepreneurs in 26 developing countries.

- The WomenConnect Challenge: Seeks to grow women's access to digital technology and bridge the digital gender divide.

- The 2X Women's Initiative: Aimed at mobilizing $1 billion in capital to support women living in the developing world. This initiative has already mobilized more than $140 million from the private sector to support women in Latin America and the Caribbean.

Black Americans

Black Americans have a true champion in President Trump.

- President Trump has created an astonishing 1.6 million new jobs for black Americans since his election. o In December, the black unemployment rate was at 5.9%.

- The black American unemployment rate has been at or below 7% for 23 consecutive months.

- Prior to President Trump's administration, the black unemployment rate had never dipped below 7%.

- In 2019, the African American unemployment rate hit a record low and remained below 7% for the entire year.

- Under President Trump, incomes for black Americans have increased by 2.6%.

- Under the Trump Economy, wages are continuing to rise, which significantly benefits the lowest-paid workers.

- The poverty rate among black Americans is at its lowest level in history.

- Under President Trump, 350,000 fewer black Americans are living in poverty.

- During the President's first year in office, the black American poverty rate fell to 21.2% down from 22% the year before.

- As a result of the historic Tax Cuts and Jobs Act, nearly 9,000 Opportunity Zones were created in all 50 states, D.C., and five territories. o Opportunity Zones which will create jobs and spur investment in disadvantaged communities. o These Opportunity Zones will spur $100 billion in private capital investment and impact 1.4 million minority households.

- President Trump signed the historic FIRST STEP Act into law.

- The FIRST STEP ACT has been widely hailed as the most meaningful criminal justice reform in a generation.

- This landmark legislation included necessary reforms to our justice system, improves our prison system, and prepares inmates for reentry in our communities.

- As a result of the First Step Act, more than 3,000 Americans have been released from prison, and 90% of those who have had their sentences reduced are black Americans.

- The First Step Act shortens mandatory minimum sentences for nonviolent drug crimes and provides judges greater liberty to go around mandatory minimums.

- The law also allows offenders sentenced under racially motivated mandatory minimums to petition for their cases to be re-evaluated.

- President Trump was awarded the 2019 Bipartisan Justice award by the nonprofit 20/20 Bipartisan Justice Center. The President received this award for his "ability to work across the aisle to achieve meaningful progress in reforming our criminal justice system."

- President Trump has committed his Administration to advance second chance hiring for former prisoners. This includes launching a "Ready to Work Initiative."

- The Trump Administration has fought for a federal tax credit on donations that fund scholarships to private schools, a proposal supported by 64% of African Americans.

- President Trump has made supporting Historically Black Colleges and Universities (H.B.C.U.s) a top priority.

- In February 2017, President Trump announced the President's Board of Advisors on H.B.C.U.s.

- The President signed an Executive Order on H.B.C.U.s in February 2017, the earliest any President has signed an Order on H.B.C.U.s.

- The E.O. established an Interagency Working Group to advance and coordinate work regarding H.B.C.U.s.

- The federal H.B.C.U. Initiative office was moved back into the White House, a move that leaders had requested under President Obama.

- President Trump has appropriated more money than any other president to H.B.C.U.s.

- The President signed legislation to increase federal funding for H.B.C.U.s by 13%, the highest level ever.

- President Trump signed the FUTURE Act into law. The law permanently funds H.B.C.U.s and simplifies the FAFSA application.

- The President worked with Congress to lift the ban on Pell Grants on summer classes.

- Through the Capital Financing Program, the Administration has provided more than $500 million in loans to H.B.C.U.s.

- The President directed the entire federal government to develop a strategy to support H.B.C.U.s. To date, this has been supported by 32 departments and agencies.

- The Administration has forgiven more than $300 million in outstanding debt for four schools impacted by natural disasters. The budget provided $10 million to defer loan payments for six schools facing financial difficulties.

- The Department of Education worked with H.B.C.U.s to protect $80 million in Title III carryover funding.

- President Trump took a big step to end discriminatory restrictions to prevent faith-based H.B.C.U.s from accessing federal support.

- The Administration continues to work with H.B.C.U.s to expand apprenticeship opportunities, career choices, and ensure they are receiving adequate support.

Latino Americans

Under President Trump's leadership, the Latino American community has thrived.

- Under President Trump, Latino Americans have experienced record low unemployment.

- More than 2.9 million jobs have been created for Latino Americans since the President was elected.

- In December, the Latino American unemployment rate was at a near-record low of 4.2%.

- The Hispanic American unemployment rate hit several record lows in 2019, including falling below 4% for the first time in history.

- The median Latino American income rose by $1,786 during President Trump's first year in office.

- In 2017, the median Latino American income hit its highest ever recorded level ($50,486).

- Since taking office, the Latino American homeownership rose by more than a percentage point (46.3% to 47.4%).

- In addition to the booming economy, President Trump renegotiated freer and fairer trade deals such as the U.S.M.C.A.

- President Trump has stood up to socialism and communism in Venezuela, Cuba, and Nicaragua.

- Thanks to pressure from President Trump, 50 countries followed President Trump's leadership in recognizing Juan Guaidó as the legitimate leader of Venezuela.

- The Trump administration has rolled back President Obama's disastrous rapprochement with Cuba, which only benefited the country's dictatorship instead of its people.

- At the direction of President Trump, the Treasury Department has imposed sanctions against senior officials in the Nicaraguan regime for their role in human rights abuses and undermining democracy.

- The President has made it clear that American interests do not align with failed socialist policies.

Asian Americans

Under President Trump's leadership, Asian American unemployment has reached record lows.

- In December, the Asian American unemployment rate was 2.5%, near a historic low.

- The lowest ever record unemployment rate for Asian Americans (2.1%) came in June 2019.

Chapter 11
Rulers

Each organization needs to accomplish objectives, and that is done solely through acquiring power. The more power any person possesses, the greater will be the influence that makes any goal more likely to be accomplished. In short, the ability to control an environment and dictate outcomes is the main reason for pursuing power. This term has many aspects when it comes to the meaning, such as it implies granted authority, actions, the properties of matter or energy, and ideas and intuitions. The most common meaning, however, is that it can make something happen.

It is in our nature to obtain as much power and control as possible. We want to run things exactly how we like it, without following the advice from professionals. We are often considered complex entities, and if we get more power, we will be more aware of what we can do, which is dangerous. It is all but guaranteed that groups, systems, or individuals that possess more power than they can control or responsibly put into use can do greater damage than anyone can imagine. Socialism believes that responsibility can only come with power, and it is important to have it as we learn how to use it to benefit the population. This refers to the legal decisions of production and distribution to be given entirely to the state government. They are the bosses, and they will be the only group to discuss, create, and release not just the output of the goods and services but also their pricing levels. Moreover, they are more than happy with that system because if the higher authority controls their products, then it makes for equal distribution and more reasonable society.

The system of production strongly goes against the idea of capitalism. If we revisit the definition of capitalism in the previous chapters, it talks about how the entire ideology is based on private ownership. This means that the production of goods and services will only be based on the market economy agenda. The market economy agenda focuses on the goods and services to be based on supply and demand in the market instead of central planning.

Capitalism is commonly known as laissez-faire, which stands for, free market. The country's political system has given a free hand to the private individuals to determine what to produce, what to sell, where to invest, and what prices they want to set to exchange goods and services. In addition to this agenda, the free market capitalism works without any limitations like an ongoing check or control of any kind. However, it is said that free-market capitalism is the only solution to the problems faced in economic production and distributions of resources. Moreover, when it comes to economic planning, capitalism prefers voluntary or decentralized decisions such as re-homesteading abandoned property and inheritance.

Thus, in simple words, the two gigantic systems can be categorized as one that hands the power to the government, while the other hands over the power to its people.

It was always going to be about power and who it would belong to get out of the day to day problems. As you will read in the previous chapters about the downfall of socialism, you will also come across why this system was one of the worst in history during the World Wars.

The Communist Manifesto of Karl Marx and Friedrich Engels proudly and convincingly talked about the importance of a classless society. It was a society where every person would contribute according to his or her skill and capability. However, they would receive rewards according to their needs, instead of how much they contributed. This caused a huge problem as the phase of difficulties occurred, and socialism was now a curse for some people.

It was unfortunate for Karl Marx, the man who brought the ideology forward, not to see his vision take place before his eyes. It was Vladimir Lenin who brought in the true impact of socialism in 1917 through the October Revolution in Russia that inaugurated the Communist Party by defying the imperial rule. With this milestone in the Soviet Union's history, socialism began to spread across the borders of Asia and Latin America.

Just like any misleading leaders of socialism, not every word or vision of Engels and Marx was implemented. Rulers like Stalin, Mao, Castro, and many others had called their governments socialist, but these rulers never followed the vision of socialism by the book. And as history has taught us, when you do not follow everything by the book and ideas of the pioneers who thought long and hard of the pros and cons of their system, there will be consequences. And, as much as they tried to ignore those consequences from happening, it affected the entire nation and brought tears and death to millions of people in the countries that adopted socialism. It is safe to say that they were never the most inspirational leaders in the history of their respective countries. They were indeed rulers and dictators. In this entire book, you will see the names of Stalin and Mao repeated on more than one occasion because it was during their dictatorships that the most powerful countries of today faced a period that nearly made them extinct. It was only because of their leader's techniques and ideas that violence and numerical games would become the only way to power.

Although there is no denying that the Soviet Union, Cuba, China, and other Nordic countries saw the best and worst times in their history, it is important to remember that the leaders believed in the best for their countries during that time.

On the one hand, it was impossible for any other nation to take them over, but on the other hand, they were breaking the country's peace from the inside. Stalin may have had a worse ruling regime than Lenin, and Mao Zedong enjoyed success in transforming China, but it was their style of ruling that differentiated the Soviet Union and China from each other and from the Nordic countries.

A closer look at these socialist countries reveals the

glaring difference in their styles of governance. The violent nature was cut down drastically in Nordic countries, and they began to adapt to a more citizen-friendly regime. The Nordic countries have a balanced tax system and a government that lives in the future to abide by the citizens' comfort through a combination of ideologies. With a combination displayed by these countries, socialist rulers would have become 'friendlier' because of the power they possessed.

Power in the political arena can be compared to fire. A fire can be very useful in so many ways, but in the wrong hands, it will be dangerous to everyone around it. Powerful individuals may depend on their own sense of ethics in making a decision. If they are already less restrained and more biased to think of sinister ways, they have a higher chance of doing something unlawful or hazardous that affect negotiations or damage their reputations.

The same is the case for the governments of today. They have the most power, and they are the ones that tell us what is good and what is not. As ordinary people, we have no other choice but to live by the system and in an environment where we are made to suffer and triumph without any of them being stable. There is nobody else to blame besides us because we are the ones that give too much power to our governments, more than they deserve. By using the United States of America as an example, the Founding Fathers had established freedom of speech, religion, bearing arms, refraining from self-incrimination, and, most importantly, equality in society. This gave the citizens the freedom and the opportunity to make the government accountable to them instead of the other way around. It was the citizens' freedom that sustained a system like that for more than a couple of centuries until they gave that power to the governmental bodies.

It is not fair to see that the government has the power to dictate to a citizen where they can or cannot live. One of the main reasons for people to move around the states is because of the differences in their tax rates. It becomes impossible to live in a certain area because of the high income and property taxes. You will hear many people say that "tax is the power to destroy," and we can see that happening when we think about the dangers of handing over power to the government. The original idea was for citizens to have the right to choose without being comprehensively stressed by governmental bodies. This was never the plan of the Founding Fathers.

Each country had tried to push its people to the point of slavery in the early centuries, but not literally. Some had practiced the system where slavery was quite common. Some countries and their governments were just being cruel.

During the 18th century, Britain saw the best times as a whole, but the citizens' anger grew as the years passed. Britain saw two different lifestyles during that era where the rich were getting richer, and the poor were getting poorer. The latter suffered because of the revolution that was taking place in the country as machines were replacing their labor. When the population was growing, and jobs were scarce, there was a great deal of tension just to earn a living. Moreover, most of the population was leaning more toward the poor rather than to the rich, where half of the poor children out of 1000 died before they turned 2-years-old due to poor hygiene and malnutrition.

It was during the 18th century that the citizens of Britain began to voice their frustrations and anger over the situation surrounding many things. It was mostly directed toward the British electoral system, and in 1832, the Parliament passed a law that changed it in the people's favor. It was called the Great Reform Act. The Act of 1832 was a conservative measure that was designed to harmonize the interests of the upper and middle-class while continuing the practice of electing the people in charge of the land for the work they did, but it also paved the way for male suffrage.

It was about time that the people would get tired of the injustice being done, so they claimed to bring a reform that would be balanced and fair. Almost everyone was disapproving the electoral system because it was easy for candidates to buy votes due to the absence of a secret ballot and the presence of a handful of voters. In addition to the electoral system that elected two M.P.s, some major towns were left with no M.P.s to represent them in the elections.

It is important to remember that if anyone out of the government tried to defy their power, it was not going to be a walk in the park to pass a Reform bill like that. This was rejected twice before becoming an official law of the country. After the second rejection, all hell broke loose when people began to riot and cause serious disturbances in the cities of Birmingham, London, Derby, Nottingham, Sherborne, Leicester, Yeovil, Exeter, and Bristol. The most notorious incident took place in Bristol, where they burned homes and buildings, killing 12 people in the process and causing around £300,000 of damage. This was enough to instill fear in the government and make them think about a reform to calm the situation down. Although the reform did not bring a permanent end to the protests, it was enough to bring the lower class into the electoral system while the towns began to have M.P.s.

Karl Marx always believed that a mass movement of the workers like a march could be the only way to achieve a truly socialist society. That is where the entire problem began as it misled people to think that the impure force was the only way for the transformation to take place. Not only was it wrong to bring a change, but it was also the root of disagreement and producing more and more socialist parties. While capitalism had the right-wingers and left-wingers, socialism also had a violent and less violent group of reformers that were dedicated to bringing the best to the struggling countries.

The differences were always pointing to the problem that people faced, especially when it came to education, health, and social status. Time and time again, they continued to remind the people that socialism only focuses on equality, which was entirely the opposite of what was being practiced.

This caused socialists to be divided. On the one hand, revolutionary socialists believed in the control of most of the private properties for the betterment of the public and social improvement. On the other hand, revisionist socialists only wanted to impose taxes and focus on public spending on the redistribution of wealth in society.

Regardless of the past, and the misleading example of socialism, freedom of speech is more important than anything else in modern times. If we go back to the Founding Fathers, they were always in favor of what the citizens needed and what they liked about the system. The country, after all, was a land for them to live and grow in. Just like any home, there needs to be a set of rules as well as a governing body to overlook all the activities that are going on and how they affect every citizen. The same is true for the government of the country as they make rules and make sure they are followed while trying to bring a balance in the financial sector.

It is clear by now that when freedom and transparency of political activities are subdued, bad things are bound to happen. It just does not affect one city but the entire country. That is when you see civil wars and riots taking place more frequently than expected. As much as governments try to avoid coming across any of it, they just happen.

Citizens are not called citizens anymore, but rather they are called subjects who are under the rule of the authority and have no escape from it. Yet, the government releases countless policies and amendments and claim that it is for the betterment of the citizens. The more we dive deeper into the problems that occur every now and then, especially behind the scenes, the more we will realize that socialism is not going to be the solution to any country's depression phase. In fact, it just causes more animosity between the people and the government. Thus, it has become more than a plea to give back the freedom of speech to the citizens from the government's hands.

Chapter 12
The Enemy-Turned-Friend of Environment

"The Earth will not continue to offer its harvest, except with faithful stewardship. We cannot say we love the land and then take steps to destroy it for use by future generations."

-John Paul II

Our planet is at the threshold of an unembellished environmental crisis. To be unaware that our environment is on a cycle that constantly changes is no longer believable. All of us are being made aware of the things that are happening around us through news channels and editorial pieces. As you read this, there is already a subtle change that is taking place around you, and nobody knows exactly what is being affected.

As the environment changes, we need to become more attentive to the problems that are causing it. Different types of weather patterns and an unexpected flood of natural disasters look to be just the beginning of the damage to our planet. At the moment, global warming has become the biggest problem of our existence because nobody wants to live on a planet melting away.

Big or small, every ecosystem is facing one kind of environmental problem or another, whereas some landscapes are altering from what we once knew. We have been exposed to many disasters than ever before. There is no better time for the people of our planet to be alert of what environmental problems exist than right now. If not, we are all doomed before we are even prepared to take our first steps of prevention.

The Ongoing Environmental Problems

As of today, 15 problems are affecting our generation, and little is done to prevent them from taking full control over the world. While it makes sense for humanity to move forward and make lives easier for the coming generation, it doesn't make sense for humanity to do it in a harmful way.

At the end of the day, we won't have a future to look forward to, let alone prepare for. Scientists are still trying to determine major environmental issues. I have prepared a list of a few of these below.

1. Pollution
2. Global Warming
3. Overpopulation
4. Natural Resource Depletion
5. Waste Disposal
6. Climate Change
7. Loss of Diversity
8. Deforestation
9. Ocean Acidification
10. Ozone Layer Depletion
11. Acid Rain
12. Water Pollution
13. Urban Sprawl
14. Public Health Issues
15. Genetic Engineering

These problems pile up and gradually affect even the most thriving countries, so nobody is safe. It takes more than a million years for the environment to recoup from air, water, and soil pollution, which is caused by gases from vehicles, oil spills, and industrial wastes, respectively. Greenhouse gases cause global warming, and so on.

Thus, we, and the government that we elect cause all of these problems. On the other hand, without government

support, no steps can be taken, and our obligation to care for the world means nothing.

Now, the government is fully involved in bringing a change in the environment. But when it comes to the rivalry of capitalism vs. socialism, the latter's supporters waste no time in giving their judgment and verdict on which one is causing more harm to the environment.

The Claims That Capitalism Is Not the Solution Some claim that socialism is the only logical solution to climate change. According to John Molyneux, an editor of the

Irish Marxist Review, without the occurrence of large-scale public ownership, the laws of capitalism will not just dominate but also have a very harmful result for the environment. He believes that public ownership should not be limited to small businesses but must be extended to banks, industries, and corporations as well.

Moreover, John also believes that an elected representative that has a democratic plan for the society and economy should head schools, hospitals, and other major workplaces. Many socialists have said that capitalism may be a way of generating more wealth, but it comes at an expense. The real concern is that in order to generate energy, fossil fuels need to be burned. Every product that is manufactured leaves behind a gigantic amount of waste. When fossil fuels are burned, they release carbon dioxide and various other greenhouse gases that heat up the planet. These are just some of the most general concerns that any ordinary person would have.

Capitalism Is the LEED-ing Movement

Burning things, emitting gases into the atmosphere, and knowing that they are of the worst kind is something all of us learn at school, and we remember it very clearly. However, I want to bring to everyone's attention that these arguments and facts, like what John has talked about in the previous points, are based on a country practicing only a single system.

Countries, as I have mentioned in the previous chapters in the book, are mixing up two economic systems to be safe. Governments control our economy, and the economy controls our environment. The land, raw material stock, and water are considered as important inputs in the production line. With a couple of things from that list varying from nation to nation, it is bound to affect any country's economy. For example, one country can have an unlimited supply of minerals, while another country has a pasturable land.

As of late, governments worldwide are trying to make their respective homelands as beautiful and safe as possible to attract tourism and business, which greatly affects the economy. For instance, for them to do that, they need to focus on planting trees, since they are very helpful in contributing to saving the climate from being harmed by carbon dioxide. If they don't, they will remain in debt by taking loans from bigger countries and becoming prone to dropping the economy's standards in order to stay afloat.

Therefore, if the economy fails, environmental deterioration rises. The government that practices a capitalist approach will find that the solution is capitalism, after all.

Capitalists also agree that pollution has increased in number with the implementation of capitalism, but they don't entirely blame it on the system, unlike the socialists. In fact, there is a positive aspect in a system that the governing bodies of the nations of the world are currently discussing in boardrooms. The truth is that capitalism is a force that can act quickly to address climate change problems before its current state becomes impossible to change. Those companies that practiced capitalism saw a big reduction in toxins and an increase in human health. One of the best examples of the private sector is when Rick Fedrizzi, in 1993, founded the U.S. Green Building Council. It is an organization that is based on the non-profit ideology and dedicates its efforts towards providing sustainability to building design, construction, and operation.

The U.S. Green Building Council created a movement that has worked marvelously to achieve water and energy efficiency, recycled materials, and indoor environmental quality. This movement was known as Leadership in Energy and Environmental Design; in short, LEED. It took just 15 years to have LEED impact 150 countries as well as register and certify 14 billion square feet of real estate under its name. With so many countries in its record, the list does include some iconic structures of the world. Therefore, reducing 21% of energy consumption from some of the biggest buildings in the world means LEED managed to save just as much energy as those released by more than 40,000 cars every year. By using green buildings such as the U.S. Green Building Council as inspiration, schools and factories have taken the step to enroll with LEED. Those that did saw a big reduction in cost and energy, while business and company buildings saw a greater return on investment. In addition to one of the biggest problems besides getting a decent return on investment, the USGBC has also allowed 2.3 million Americans to find employment. With each year passing, the numbers are sure to double because of how profitable green buildings have become since 2011.

It was just the start of something remarkable for the world. The USGBC gave every type of platform a chance to save as much as possible when nobody thought there was a way. United Technologies, for example, saw its stock price doubled; they saved 30% on gas emissions and 33% on water use. Being one of the world's biggest manufacturing powerhouses and saving in such amounts is a big deal. Likewise, Unilever saved 37% on gas emissions and helped the company save around $422 million.

Companies Promote Environmental Friendliness

It was a couple of generations ago where it looked like the world's resources were unlimited, and people only had to use them not only in the right way to form their outline for their ventures but also to grow humanity. When we look at it today, we are left to wonder how drastically the tables have turned. People are looking for new resources and ways to protect them.

Times have also changed from the way the world views capitalism. Through the LEED movement, a handful number of giant corporations are wasting less and earning more. In the coming years, others like them are definitely joining the flow. World leaders are setting up meetings to work together on some of the 15 environmental problems that I stated previously. As of today, 11 top companies have taken a step to fight climate change.

1. Panasonic
2. New Belgium Brewing Company
3. Walmart
4. Apple
5. Ikea

6. IBM

7. Unilever

8. Chipotle

9. Biogen

10. ChicoBag

11. Carbon Lighthouse

By using the LEED module, **Panasonic** shifted its office from Secaucus, NJ, to downtown Newark next to the Newark Penn Station. Its employees were allowed to travel via the station, which led to 50% of the workers to stop coming to work by car.

New Belgium Brewing Company focused on always being eco-friendly because it required more energy to make beer. While anyone else would be the first to tell you that it is not a good idea to have a beer company, they proved everyone wrong. The company has many options to generate power. For example, they use solar panels for the bottling plant and an anaerobic digester for the brewing. They have also given bicycles to their employees to travel around the site.

Walmart is a name that many would not have expected to land on the list. Nevertheless, the decision to bring in organic products and sell them at a reasonable price paid off. They came into the public eye and continued the process by replacing dangerous chemicals with safer ones. This led the organic farming department to flourish and be better known worldwide.

When anyone mentions **Apple**, people already know the impact it has had on the world with innovations. They have a solar farm that is dedicated to their power operations and uses an alternate of paper for packaging their products to save the trees. In doing so, they were one of the few companies to stand against climate denialism.

Ikea has focused on buying renewable energy and solar panels to provide power to its branches and offices nationwide. It did not stop there. The products Ikea sold were vegan Swedish meatballs, which caught the eye of every member who tried the original recipe. In addition, they had cotton that was made from less water, fertilizers, and chemicals.

In one way or another, IBM, Unilever, Chipotle, Biogen, and **ChicoBag** have stood against climate change to deal with problems like deforestation, greenhouse gas emissions, sourcing resources from humanely treated farms, and finding ways to recycle the waste. This was done to show every other competitor that business success and saving the environment should not compete against each other.

While these companies are moving around on the list of which is the environment's best friend, another company is silently working toward the same goal and giving an incentive for its customers.

The company goes by the name of Carbon Lighthouse and is co-founded by Brenden Millstein and Raphael Rosen. The main problem that these two individuals saw was that the biggest companies promised a lot of results but gave nothing and charged customers a hefty fee. In short, customers were not getting what they paid for, and that was becoming a huge financial problem for every investor.

For any startup, there needs to be a business model that makes the company unique and captivating to invest in. Thus, Millstein says, *"We innovate first and foremost by the way our contracts are structured. We charge a fixed monthly fee, require no upfront investments, and we guarantee a minimum amount of savings for the customer. If the actual savings are higher than that, our customers keep that difference. If they are lower, Carbon Lighthouse writes a check to cover the difference."*

Moreover, according to Millstein, the best way to deal with the problems of climate change is to focus on accountability and profitability. As I have mentioned earlier, Carbon Lighthouse has Tesla's backing, and the company has already used Carbon's services and can vouch for their business model.

By now, you already understand that when businesses move toward the 'green side,' they have a positive influence on the environment. Sustainable practices such as the nature of work done by Carbon Lighthouse and other companies can reduce costs and incentivize individuals to adopt eco-friendly living.

Every company has a set of plans that have to affect the company's impact on the environment and the costs. More importantly, every company needs a team of skilled and hardworking employees to see them past every competitor. In this way, they need to encourage rather than inspire their workers to work more, but very few encourage saving the planet.

Those companies that encourage saving the planet make sure to focus on educating their team and reveal everything about global warming and being energy efficient. The companies also provide incentives such as giving a small reward, which can be monetary or non-monetary like a plaque. A gesture like this will encourage employees to work harder on being green. Moreover, to bring a little fun to it, companies would normally have groups and competitions. Often, some employees believe that this is just part-time. However, when they see their managers or owners practicing it or find out that they have been practicing it for years, they also decide to get involved and form a team of their own.

While I suggest that every multinational company should have a Green Team within their offices, it is also important for them to have accurate information to get results in this respect. Each step can make or break their cause, and that will affect the planet more. Thus, getting everyone involved in making the planet safer and greener must be an obligation of every employee and every citizen. Capitalism is the key to solving environmental concerns; it is up to business people to use it wisely.

Chapter 13
The Roots of Capitalism

The official system of capitalism developed in the 16th century, but its roots can be traced back to the Middle Ages in Europe. That was when profits and capital started being used to increase production instead of being spent on unprofitable things. In those times, when the rich accumulated more wealth while the poor suffered, it justified the belief that the richer worked harder and more than the less privileged.

Capitalism is an economic ideology that liberates the market, so the production and profits are owned and collected privately. The production follows the guidelines of the market alone and distributes the income amongst those who operate it. One thing that contributed to the rise of the capitalist economy was when the supply of European precious metals increased. The prices inflated, but the wages did not. Through the mercantilist era during 1500-1750, capitalists enjoyed how the national power of some states provided the perfect social conditions that helped the economy grow. Legal codes and uniform monetary systems allowed for the market to move toward a more private ownership system. Then, during the 18th century, capitalism spread to the industry. Profits and capital accumulated during the previous years were invested in the technological progress of industries. Adam Smith described classic capitalism as letting markets that were self-regulatory have the freedom to make economic choices and decisions freely. After the French Revolution annihilated the last bits of feudalism to nothing, the country began to follow Smith's capitalist policies and ideas even more.

In the 19th century, industrial capitalism brought forth a factory system that created a class of industrial workers who lived in poor conditions. That inspired the philosophy from Karl Marx that proposed a different view from capitalism. Marx's proposed philosophy followed the model that allowed governments to control and dictate to the people – what they can or cannot do through taxation, regulations, codes, courts, etc.

Capitalism brought people the liberty to take control of their lives and capital, but Marx predicted that the working class would overthrow capitalism. And though after World War I, the world market suffered, and trade barriers developed, and the Great Depression of the 1930s created support for socialism, the decades after World War II changed everything. Different capitalist countries and economies started improving, and by the time the 1970s rolled around, capitalism had found its significant and permanent role in society. The people of those times made great industrial moves that helped the economies grow rapidly. People's faith in capitalism was restored once again.

The recent Great Recession, however, has ruined the reputation of capitalism and made the younger generation think it is some evil philosophy that has wrecked society when that couldn't be farther from the truth. Capitalism follows the democratic and moral values on which we can build a free society. It is the single most successful economic philosophy that has provided much progress and growth for the people.

Capitalism is unpredictable and disruptive. People regard it as something that breeds the selfish desires of humans. However, capitalism follows the most moral values, such as hard work, devotion, charity, and generosity. How capitalism favors humanity, and the development of the economy is through creatively destroying the older industries to make way for the new ones. Everyone knows how you need something to break so you can get the latest version. If older versions of industries or products didn't get destroyed, how would humanity progress to better and improved versions of it? It gives capitalism the bad reputation of taking away jobs from the poor and giving them to wealthy ones who don't deserve it. But by proceeding to a more modern era and setting up industries that meet the demands of time, capitalism creates new opportunities and jobs. And if the poor do not get those jobs, it is only because they do not have the skills for them.

Another common mentality is the one that follows the phrase "rich get richer, and the poor get poorer." People think because of capitalism, the rich keep accumulating more wealth by taking advantage of the poor and labor class. They think the rich get richer at the expense of the poor and are privileged because of their wealth, while the poor keep suffering at their hands. But what they do not realize is that the rich cannot get richer without the poor. And the rich drive the economy towards progress and growth. The rich only get richer by investing in newer industries and ventures that grow to benefit the people. They invest in small businesses, which then grow into bigger and more successful ones thanks to the excess capital being invested in their production. When the rich earn profits through those investments, they use that capital to purchase goods and services that provide a smooth flow of supply and demand that helps the economy grow. The aristocracy is not a fixed group of people. Otherwise, the economy would remain stagnant and never grow or increase. If we want the economy to grow, we should allow people to get rich and earn money.

People think governmental laws and regulations controlling the markets and economy are necessary to protect the people and the goods. Even though some laws help democratic capitalism function successfully, others do more harm than good. These regulations are created by political constituencies that are only interested in their selfish political gains. They meddle with the successful and innovative flow of the economy and its growth. Trying to manage the economy only proves to be hurting the people they promise to protect.

"It has been said that democracy is the worst form of government except all the others that have been tried."

-Winston Churchill.

If a government were to get involved with the economy and its matters, we could run into many problems such as corruption, dissemination of wrong information, and the lack of incentives for innovation. Having the government in control can lead people to manipulate the economy for their own political agendas and then spread incorrect or incomplete information.

Capitalism ensures that resources are distributed based on how much someone deserves it or has worked for it. In the market, it only allocates resources to those industries or products the consumers prefer. It means that those who manufacture goods that aren't good enough according to the people do not get rewarded by getting resources they don't deserve.

Capitalism also makes sure that productivity remains optimum. Industries cut down on costs to increase their productivity and improve efficiency. That allows them to remain in business because if they do not make changes accordingly or upgrade as per the market demands, then they can run out of business.

Capitalism ensures that it meets the needs and demands of consumers. Industries keep on the lookout for changes and new trends in the market. They analyze the market to see what the consumers are most attracted to and what they demand the most. It ensures that consumers' preferences are always met, and the trends are followed by the firms diligently.

Capitalism provides incentives for firms and entrepreneurs, as well. Economies grow based on the opportunity for financial growth and gain. If there weren't any chances for financial gain, people wouldn't set up industries or businesses hoping to earn large profits. When faced with the chance of financial gain, everyone works twice as hard. The incentive to earn money or more money makes people efficient and simultaneously work hard. If they weren't promised financial rewards, no one would take the risk of initiating startups.

Joseph Aloïs Schumpeter was an Austrian economist who talked about "creative destruction" extensively. In fact, he was the one who coined the term and brought forth the idea in 1942. Joseph said that one of the most powerful arguments for capitalism was creative destruction. According to him, the industries and firms that are outdated go out of business because consumers have moved on to bigger and better things. If that means a loss of jobs, it also means a new opportunity. People can find better jobs and opportunities in newer ventures and better fields.

We can achieve economic freedom only through capitalism. And economic freedom can bring about political freedom too. A state that regulates or limits individuals from the right to own businesses or where they can work will face the public's intervention. Even though it cannot guarantee it, economic freedom can be the start of political freedom.

Speaking about morals, capitalism is the best in that case because it follows the code of no discrimination. Capitalism encourages trade with every willing nation. That means going past racial, national, and language barriers for the betterment of your economy. In a capitalist state, racial or any other discrimination wouldn't be accepted because whoever hinders the process of trade would face penalties by the state. Firms would look past sectarian differences between nations for the sake of growth and progress of the economy.

Being able to own your own assets and not have them regulated by the government is an idea that has been accepted and supported by many. Capitalism gives people the right to own and set up their businesses based on their wishes without government interference. You control how you do business without governmental supervision. Income gets determined by market forces instead of redistributing it in the hands of someone who didn't work as hard as others. It means a fair distribution of income based on market statistics.

Capitalism promises that the pure and direct process of supply and demand would determine prices. If there is more demand, the prices would be high, but if the consumers don't want a product, then it won't cost as much. Market incentives help give firms the motivation to work more efficiently. Firms cut costs to improve efficiency because it is what the market dictates.

In the 1800s, Karl Marx came to consider religion as the source of people's pain, which is an unfair economic system. He accused religion of being the opium of the population, diverting them from freeing themselves from oppressive systems. Yet capitalism has successfully compromised religion by reliably committing that the future will, in fact, be materially improved, and not because of extreme intervention but because of markets made by men.

In conclusion, capitalism is a way for the economy to grow and prosper because state-regulated economies are less efficient since they provide fewer incentives. Capitalism provides the ideal opportunity for the economy to become dynamic by improving the efficiency and productivity of firms and industries. It provides incentives that allow many industries to grow to unthinkable heights, which a state ruled economy would never allow. Capitalism allows for the economy to grow and progress rapidly with the help of inventions that make industries grow.

People look down on capitalism and yet hold democracy to a higher standard. This is ironic because they both follow the same moral principle. Capitalism and democracy allow people the freedom and right to choose what they produce or purchase. That is a high moral principle because it empowers the people instead of taking away their power by giving control over to the state. People say that businesspeople are not reliable because they have a selfish financial agenda. But with democracy, politicians also promise a lot for their own political agenda. No matter how many promises your political leader makes, and the state provides initiatives that seem to benefit the people, it still might not work out. All because of one fatal flaw – the freedom to choose. It is the same as when merciful dictators think they are better than corrupt politicians. But then again, the people are still without their basic right to choose what they buy or produce. That freedom makes or breaks the entire economy. Is it a good option if people get every facility but lose the right to choose what they consume?

The power to choose what you consume or produce for your financial gain is one that is the most fulfilling. That is why capitalist states that have been threatened by governments that want to regulate them had revolutions, where the people overthrew the socialists in-charge. The freedom to make the choice of what an individual does with their assets and taking profits that they earned through hard work is enough for people to want to rise in the act of revolution.

Capitalism is not only the most beneficial system for a country's economy but also its people. That is why so many nations still support and function as capitalist states – because they have witnessed how their economy grew and enjoyed the various benefits of capitalism and the liberties it provides them.

Chapter 14
The Death of American Freedom

"The American Dream is about Freedom."

–Nancy Pelosi

The Concept of Neoliberalism

The American Dream is the most sought-after ambition in the world as it stems from our basic rights. This basic right allows us to perform any action or task to attain stability in our livelihoods. At the same time, through this right, we can understand ourselves more innately and discern right from wrong.

This basic right is none other than freedom of speech and action, and through it, countless Americans have established their presence in the country. Through this right, Americans have completely changed their life patterns and become a part of numerous rags to riches stories. This is the role of freedom in American society, and sadly, it has been changed into something entirely different. As opposed to the ideals and message conveyed by freedom, modern Americans have been at the mercy of a completely different system. As a matter of fact, this system has been in place for a considerable amount of time and has greatly influenced the modern world. This system is referred to as neoliberalism, and it evolved from the 20th-century resurgence of 19th-century ideas associated with laissez-faire economic liberalism.

In addition to this, free-market capitalism also played a major role in the development of neoliberalism. As a result of free-market capitalism, society has undergone a paradigm shift away from the post-war Keynesian accord. This prior consensus had lasted from 1945 all the way to 1980. And, after the advent of neoliberalism, the socio-economic system had greatly shifted their policies and norms.

To put it in simple terms, Neoliberalism is mainly related to policies of economic liberalization. These policies consist of privatization, deregulation, free trade, austerity, and reductions in government spending. The sole purpose of these policies and strategies is to substantially elevate the influence of the private sector in a country's economy and society at large. Still, with time, the main attributes of neoliberalism in thought and practice have been the subject of immense debate by scholars and other political intellectuals. Looking back, the official term of *"neoliberalism"* didn't commence up until the early 20th century. And, back then, neoliberalism had a plethora of different meanings. However, its meaning became well-defined and more prevalent during the 1970s and 1980s. In fact, neoliberalism was even used by various scholars of different schools of social sciences. Neoliberalism has also been a well-studied subject of critics.

However, this term is infrequently utilized by advocates of free-market policies. The case being that neoliberalism means different things to different people. Some scholars even claim that neoliberalism has *"mutated"* into geopolitically distinct hybrids. This is the case because its policies have traveled far and wide, reaching millions of people in a matter of decades. People can even say that neoliberalism shares many attributes with other concepts that have disputed meanings, such as the likes of democracy. As an economic philosophy, neoliberalism surfaced through the efforts of European liberal scholars in the 1930s. These scholars and intellectuals originally wanted to replenish and renew central ideas from classical liberalism and make them relevant today. They did this because they felt that the ideas were plummeting in popularity. Moreover, these ideas had been overtaken by the urge to control markets. This was because the world had entered a time following the Great Depression. And, because of this, the philosophy had manifested in policies specifically designed to counter the volatility of free markets. By doing this, the concerned country could significantly alleviate the subsequent negative social consequences and stabilize their economy. All in all, the original drive for this development arose from a need to prevent repeating the economic failures of the early 1930s. Many scholars claim to this day that this mindset had given birth to classical liberalism's fundamental economic policies and strategies.

About the time neoliberalism had turned into a household name in the 1980s, certain politicians had begun to use this philosophy to their benefit. Among these individuals, Augusto Pinochet's economic reforms of Chile are identified as classic representations of neoliberalism. However, because of the results of Pinochet's policies, neoliberalism had swiftly taken on undesirable connotations.

In fact, the image of neoliberalism had deteriorated to such an extent that Pinochet's example was used extensively by critics of market reform and laissez-faire capitalism. These critics had immediately begun associating neoliberalism with the theories of Mont Pelerin Society economists. These economists include the likes of Friedrich Hayek, Milton Friedman, and James M. Buchanan. In addition to economists, a number of politicians and policymakers had become the figureheads of the neoliberalism movement.

These politicians are none other than the likes of Margaret Thatcher, Ronald Reagan, and Alan Greenspan. By 1994, and with the passage of NAFTA and with the Zapatistas' reaction to Neoliberalism's development in Chiapas, the term had officially entered global circulation. Over the past few decades, think tanks, scholars, and economists have taken a keen interest in neoliberalism and are developing it with time. [1]

Neoliberalism and Socialism

---

[1] Spring et al. (2016), The Handbook of Neoliberalism. Retrieved from https://www.routledge.com/The-Handbook-of-Neoliberalism/Springer-Birch-MacLeavy/p/book/9781138844001

To sum it up, neoliberalism can be easily described as a philosophy on how a capitalist economy should be governed. However, if we were to take the case of socialism or democratic socialism, this philosophy is mainly concerned with those economies that adhere to a socialist structure. If we were to delve further into neoliberalism, we would learn that it is nothing but an upgraded version of classical liberalism. Basically, neoliberalism is a viewpoint that says free markets are the best way to distribute resources in an economy. Hence, governments or national institutions must be allowed to interfere as little as possible.

Focusing on the policy of neoliberalism, it carried directions for deregulation, privatization, free trade, small government, macroeconomic stability, strong property rights, investor protection*, and "market-led" or "market-friendly"* solutions to key political issues. To understand this concept, we can take the case of carbon trading. Carbon trading has been known to curb climate change. It does this by incentivizing greenhouse gas emitters to reduce their emissions and fund carbon repossession projects throughout the known world. Through carbon trading, we can see that the running of the government could also be carried out much like a business. Neoliberalism, as a way of handling capitalism, differs from social democracy. The case is that there is an immense role to play for the state in regulating the economy and providing welfare for its citizens.

Moreover, democratic socialism is a type of socialism that runs through a democratic form of governance. Socialism, by definition, means collective control. Socialist governments exact this control by either direct worker management or indirect state control of the various means of production. These means include capital, factories, machines, and tools. As mentioned previously, this control is only for the sole benefit of the workforce.

This fact also corresponds to the disintegration of the capital-labor class distinction and exploitative relationship. Democratic socialists believe that a system should be run democratically. They do this by liberal representative democracy. This form of democracy is present in most of the Western world. Other than this, socialists have also been known to vouch for a direct form of democracy. Based on this fact, we can determine that democratic socialists, as a way of controlling socialism, are completely separate from Leninist or Maoists. These two schools feel that an authoritarian state is necessary to achieve socialism. Therefore, it is vital to contemplate that social democracy and democratic socialism, despite sounding similar, are extremely different.[2]

The Rise of Neoliberalism

There is no doubting the fact that the post-1990 rules of globalization, supported by both conservatives and moderate liberals, are the original embodiments of neoliberalism. The original intention of Bretton Woods in 1944, which involved the use of fixed exchange rates and controls on speculative private capital and the inevitable creation of the IMF and World Bank, enabled member countries to practice national forms of managed capitalism.

This accord had, on the surface, insulated the countries from the critical and deflationary influences of short-term speculative private capital flows. However, as doctrine and power shifted in the 1970s, the IMF, the World Bank, and later even the WTO (that replaced the old GATT) had transformed into their ideological opposites. Instead of

---

[2] Ebeling (2019), Why Neo-Liberalism is Really Neo-Socialism. Retrieved from https://www.aier.org/article/why-neo-liberalism-is-really-neo-socialism/

becoming the instruments of support for mixed national economies, these organizations had turned into the enforcers of neoliberal policies.

As a matter of fact, the standard package of the *"Washington Consensus"* of approved policies for developing nations had contained demands for opening their capital markets to speculative private finance. In addition to this, the package also included the cutting of taxes on capital, flagging social transfers, and stripping labor regulation and public ownership. Nonetheless, the private capital investment in poor or developing countries proved to be fickle at the very least. In fact, the result was usually excessive inflows during the boom period of the cycle and penal withdrawals during the bust.

This was in direct opposition to the patient, long-term development capital that these countries needed, and it was even offered by the World Bank of a prior era. During the bust stage, the IMF normally executes even more stringent neoliberal demands. They do this to influence the price of financial bailouts, which includes stubborn budgetary austerity. The IMF carries out these policies allegedly to restore the confidence of the speculative capital markets that are responsible for the recurring boom-bust cycle.

Till now, numerous nations, from Latin America to East Asia, had already faced this cycle of boom, bust, and then the subsequent IMF pile-on. In fact, Greece is still suffering from the impact to this day. Following 1990, hyper-globalism also consisted of trade treaties whose terms had really benefited multinational corporations. Conventionally, trade agreements had been mostly about the reciprocal reductions of tariffs by nations. Nations were even free to have whatever brand of regulation, public investment, or social policies of their choice.

With the initiation of the WTO, several policies other than tariffs were labeled as trade-distorting. These were also referred to as takings without compensation. In addition to this, trade deals gave free access to foreign capital to dismantle national regulation and public ownership. Apart from this, special courts were developed through which foreign corporations and investors could complete end-runs around national authorities to challenge regulation for impeding commerce.[3] However, with the advent of neoliberalism, much of these economic policies and measures are overlooked by the establishment, resulting in socio-economic depravity.

---

[3] Kuttner (2019), Neoliberalism: Political Success, Economic Failure. Retrieved from https://prospect.org/economy/neoliberalism-political-success-economic-failure/

Chapter 15
The Death of American Freedom (Part II)

Neoliberalism and Income Inequality

It is important to note that, in the modern-day, the U.S. experiences significant income inequality. The main reason behind this is that the richest one percent of the population has more wealth than the bottom eighty percent. The elite class has managed to acquire tremendous wealth because of the policies initiated by neoliberalists. Many researchers and economists link the exponential increase in income inequality to the emergence of neoliberalism along with other variants of socialism.

This is largely because neoliberalism deals with the execution of policies that nationalize the concerned economy. The concept of the free market and laissez-faire economy is overlooked in neoliberalism. Instead, neoliberalism supports a system that encourages the active involvement of the government in key economic decisions. Rather than letting the market decide its future, neoliberalists believe that the government needs to interfere in certain situations. And, unfortunately, neoliberalism not only survives but thrives in America. This is the case because the idea of an economy with considerable involvement from the government or any other external party has become vital to the American identity and *"American Dream."* The American Dream is based on the belief that anyone can work their way to wealth and success. Instead of elevating every citizen's socioeconomic status, neoliberalism has caused a dramatic increase in income inequality.

This is mainly because neoliberalism ideologies only reward those who are already wealthy. It does this by providing fewer nets or advantages for poor populations to fall back on. To understand the factual failures of neoliberalism, we can take the example of an affluent American citizen. A person born into wealth and privilege may find it relatively easier to achieve a college education, have access to a resourceful network, and subsequently attain a lucrative occupation. On the contrary, people from low-income communities simply cannot avail the same financial opportunities nor advance their socioeconomic status. The poor do not receive the same aid or financial support from the government. Because of this, in times of crisis, the disenfranchised end up losing everything they have earned on their life journeys. Despite this inequality, neoliberalism and other offshoots of socialism remain popular in the United States.

While there are several reasons for this dilemma, one of the major reasons why neoliberalism has led to income inequality in the country is its acceptance as a dominant economic theory. After World War II ended, the same time when most individuals were concerned about maintaining their social security, most of the world adhered to a Keynesian or Marxist philosophy.

According to this policy, the state had to manage a significant portion of the economy, and citizens were given immense social protection. However, this so-called social protection or government control had prevented the masses from amassing any type of financial security. This is mainly because through tighter government regulations and involvement, the average person was not allowed to own and benefit from their own company. This tragedy ruined the common people and prevented them from availing their basic right: financial security. As a matter of fact, Alexander

Stille describes in *The Paradox of the New Elite*, *"just after the protest movements of the 1960s and early 1970s… think tanks dedicated to defending the free enterprise system – such as the Cato Institute and the Heritage Foundation – were born."* According to Stille, the income inequality created by communist and socialist policies had not only resulted in anarchy but eventually led to the reformation of the free market and capitalism. In addition to this, Stille, along with other veteran economists, has repeatedly stressed that if neoliberalism isn't contained or curbed, it could have disastrous implications for American society.

Along with Stille, in the book *A Short History of Neoliberalism*, Susan George reaffirms the shift of the economy and points out that, *"neoliberals have bought and paid for their own vicious and regressive 'Great Transformation'… a huge international network of foundations… [that] develop, package and push their ideas and doctrine relentlessly."* In other words, since the 1960s, it has been seen that neoliberal thinkers have utilized their wealth in a number of underhanded ways. Among these ways, the most heinous method is creating institutions that tilt the ideological perspective of the world toward a socialist society. This is a system that rewards the ruling elite and penalizes the poor in the long haul. Furthermore, neoliberals have conducted this ideological shift with such finesse that, now, neoliberalism appears to be, in the words of Susan George, *"the natural and normal condition of humankind."*

Some experts and economists infer that neoliberalism, and even socialists, for that matter, breed income inequality by nature. As a matter of fact, many recent books debate that *"the worsening income inequality is an inevitable outcome of socialism… the rise in inequality reflects markets working precisely as they should."* The key point to note from this deduction is that in a socialist society, entrepreneurs and business owners ultimately become increasingly dominant over their own labor. Moreover, the book's theory suggests that neoliberalist policies promote government regulation and enable top tier officials to run their businesses freely without scrutiny. As a result of this situation, these influential people maximize profit for themselves and their stakeholders, with no regard and consideration for their workforce. This issue becomes even more concerning for the average citizen as neoliberalism is slowly turning into the norm in global business. And, because of its policies, neoliberalism will inevitably impair the global economy beyond repair.[4]

Neoliberalism, Democratic Socialists and Bernie Sanders

Despite the well-known and apparent disadvantages of neoliberalism, certain politicians have not only adopted the system but ardently promoted its policies. These politicians are often referred to as democratic socialists. And, according to them, the roots of economic freedom and neoliberalism are two sides of the same coin.

In fact, a self-described democratic socialist, Bernie Sanders, had been an advocate for democratic socialism for quite some time. Prominent economists even hold Bernie Sanders responsible for the current term's discourse more than any other political figure. Moreover, they also consider him to be the propitiator of the country's definitional shift from a free market to a controlled economy. To put it in simple terms, Sander's brand of socialism or neoliberalism centers on New Deal politics and the Nordic Model. Sanders

---

[4] Dewey (2017), How Neoliberalism has caused income inequality. Retrieved from https://medium.com/of-course-global/how-neoliberalism-has-caused-income-inequality-9ec1fcaacb

has openly shown his support for a market economy that focuses on heavier taxation. He hopes that this taxation will inevitably facilitate wider, sturdier public provisions. According to Sanders, key social services like education, childcare, and healthcare must be under government protections and overreaching influence. He considers them to be basic rights that must be catered for by the government.

"I think that when we look at a modern, democratic, civilized society, you're looking at economic rights in addition to political freedoms," Sanders said to a local news channel. He further added that *"I happen to believe that in the year 2019, with all of the wealth around us, we can create an economy which guarantees health care to all people as a human right, which guarantees education as a right. Economic rights as human rights."* On the surface, Sanders does a remarkable job of defining his terms despite being a politician. Yet, Sanders's brand of *"democratic socialism"* stands in direct opposition to the system's inherent structure. This is the case because democratic socialism supports a society where the government owns the means of production and centrally plans the economy from top to bottom. In other words, we can safely say that this

system is nothing more than classic socialism under the banner of a democratic framework. In the eyes of his opponents and peers, Sanders advocates for what is commonly labeled as *"social democracy."* According to social democracy, a mixed economic system is where a capitalist market works as a much larger, more robust social safety net. Additionally, the market also provides social risk-sharing for its citizens.

However, in the case of Bernie Sanders, the New Deal substance may, in fact, be more important than any label he receives. Despite this situation, both the Foundation for Economic Education, an established libertarian think tank, and Jacobin, a democratic socialist magazine, have made a clear distinction between *"social democracy"* and *"democratic socialism."* This distinction needs to be present to bring clarity to the American political discourse and make the political system more unified than ever. Despite Bernie's attempt at toning down neoliberalism, his political system has yet to make a significant difference in income disparity. To make matters worse, he and his system have become a target for the current administration. This is because President Donald Trump, during his 2019 State of the Union address, had openly denounced calls to adopt *"socialism"* in the United States. As a whole, Sanders might have brought socialism back into the political landscape, but it has expanded beyond both its original definition and his own New Deal outlook. As per the outlook of many economists and politicians, Bernie Sander's system has become synonymous with inequality.

To contemplate it even further, we can refer to the rhetoric of Alexandria Ocasio-Cortez. Ocasio-Cortez's brand of democratic socialism is a bit of a moving target. This is because she, herself, admits that the term houses distinct definitions. Often, Ocasio-Cortez aligns democratic socialism directly with the Nordic Model. On the other hand, she also promotes the system as a form of economic democracy. Even if we discount these two descriptions, Ocasio-Cortez's definition of democratic socialism is extremely broad. In her definition, *she says, "Capitalism, to me, is an ideology of capital. The most important thing is the concentration of capital, and it means that we seek and prioritize profit and the accumulation of money above all else, and we seek it at any human and environmental cost… But when we talk about ideas, for example, like democratic socialism, it means putting democracy and society first, instead of capital first. For the love of capital is the root of all evil."* She further elaborates that socialism must not correspond to the fear that the government will eventually take over our businesses. However, this fear is not only present but is eating away society with the passing moment. This system supports the role of the government and completely negates the path of the free market economy.

Other than this, we have the use of socialism defined by President Trump. Just recently, Trump has aligned democratic socialism strongly to Venezuela's mismanaged economy. By doing this, President Trump is attacking Sanders and Ocasio-Cortez's versions, all the while undermining the social democracies, they drew inspiration from. In addition to this, Donald Trump has also tried to propitiate the old Cold War embers by combining socialism and communism. *"Virtually everywhere socialism or communism has been tried, it has produced suffering, corruption, and decay,"* Trump told the United Nations' General Assembly. He further stated, *"Socialism's thirst for power leads to expansion, incursion, and oppression. All nations of the world should resist socialism and the misery that it brings to everyone."* Although when describing the Nordic countries, the report claims that they *"differ significantly from what economists have in mind when they think of socialism."* As a result, Trump's utilization of the word not only reverts to the classical definition but also sets aside any post-1949 reforms and accomplishments.

Much to the frustration of sticklers and pedants all around the world, it is important to note that words change meaning consistently. This phenomenon is a natural, unavoidable part of our language, and socialism is a word undergoing the same evolution. However, the main principle, method, and ideology remain the same. All the while, the left block, and its adherents embellish the label of liberal and identify with it openly.

Just like neoliberalism, socialism is undergoing a substantial change. It is, in fact, on the road to polysemy along a plethora of party lines. In the case of Republicans, democratic socialism carries the taint of Cold War animosity and has become a widely known scorn.5 In

---

[5] Dickinson (2019), Are Bernie Sanders and Alexandria Ocasio-Cortez redefining socialism in the U.S.? Retrieved from https://bigthink.com/politics-current-affairs/bernie-sanders-socialism?rebelltitem=5#rebelltitem5

the end, the fear of socialism is mostly based on one idea. This idea is that the end of the road for the government is the totalitarian horror of the early twentieth century. There are other objections to neoliberalism and socialism as well. These objections typically involve muttered words like 'market' and 'efficiency.' However, for the fathers of neoliberalism such as Friedrich Hayek, the main fear was the ever-increasing role of the state in the economy.

According to Hayek, neoliberalism and democratic socialism were just another step towards the chimneys of Dachau. Dachau, meaning that the overall power in a country was concentrated among a know-it-all elite that is deaf to the problems facing its people. In addition to this, the system also involved the ever-present surveillance of the population, whether "suspect" or not, and a widespread, armed bureaucracy ready to stamp out dissent at all corners. The apostle John is now advanced in age, writing from Ephesus to remind and encourage the Church to remain faithful to the basics of Christianity. This system would, in turn, lead to countless bodies being locked up and tortured in prisons. In other words, it is a system that asserts the power to treat its citizens as mere subjects while demanding secrecy and impunity for itself. It wasn't just Hayek, writing in the shadow of the Second World War, who obsessed over this fear of neoliberalism. On the contrary, right-wing, anti-government rhetoric in the Obama years was filled with talk of Nazis, Hitler, and tyranny, until the very same people embraced a politician of their own in 2015. Speaking of whom, amid one of his recent anti-socialist broadsides, Trump recently stated that *"socialism eventually must always give rise to tyranny."*

This threat was halted indefinitely with the great promise of capitalism. This is mainly because, even if people might suffer from a lack of resources and die from preventable disease, they at least had all the political freedoms denied by authoritarian socialist states. It is important to note that the gulag hasn't come to Sweden or Norway. This is the case because their governments pay for people's medical bills and have minimum involvement in the economy. Furthermore, the society envisioned by socialists ultimately uproots decision-making power, whether economic or political, to working people and focuses on the state. In the present day, it is abundantly clear that more than seven decades after Hayek's worry, *"what was promised by neoliberalism as the*

Road to Freedom was, in fact, the High Road to Servitude."
In the end, neoliberalism has put us, the American People,
on the high road.

In the U.S.A., there now exists what Matt Taibbi has
accurately described as an *"authoritarian state-within-a-
state."* Tom Engelhardt has also added his cents and termed
the present government as a 'shadow government.' As per
Engelhardt, the government has the power to decide who
lives and dies based on evidence that's never seen. And,
because of this, the condemned can't challenge their
accusations.

This leads to various deaths of countless unknown people
across the globe without trial or jury, including,
sometimes, American citizens. This same shadow state
functions as a vast, global surveillance system that
collects numerous data about our intimate, private behavior.
Often, this information is collected in order to be used
against political enemies. Surprisingly enough, it wasn't a
socialist strongman who oversaw the creation of this state.
Instead, the man who presided over much of this was the

neoliberal Democrat known as Barack Obama.[6] Based on this scenario, it is high time that the U.S. government realizes its mistakes and takes a definitive step against neoliberalism. The current and future administrations need to introduce policies that subvert the government's economic hold and limit their influence on the economy. Only then will the country come out of the shadow of income inequality and embark on a path of everlasting growth and true economic freedom guaranteed by free-market capitalism.

---

[6] Marcetic (2019), The Neoliberal Road to Serfdom. Retrieved from https://www.jacobinmag.com/2019/03/neoliberalism-totalitarianism-surveillance-hayek-socialism

Chapter 16
Capitalism and its Promise to the Youth

"If you don't believe in winning, you don't believe in free enterprise, capitalism, our way of life."

–Tom Landry

After understanding the genuine threat of neoliberalism and how it is affecting the American society, we will now turn our attention towards the most efficient socioeconomic system in the world, capitalism, and what it promises to the next generation. Capitalism is the answer to every major or minor problem in American society.

Furthermore, the sooner the American youth realizes this, the better equipped they will be to handle life's pressures and challenges. The nation's youth needs to understand the foundation of this great country and look for ways to use it to improve their lives as much as possible. Ideally, the youth must understand the fundamentals of capitalism and how they can help them secure their financial freedom. There is no doubting the fact that true financial and economic freedom cannot be achieved without capitalism. Capitalism holds the key to socioeconomic equality, but it also aids people in turning their own ideas into a profitable venture. As a matter of fact, the mega-corporations, and institutions we see today could not have been possible without the advent of capitalism. Considering the capitalistic policies of the United States, numerous entrepreneurs and business professionals were able to expound on their ideas and make something truly enduring. If it had not been for capitalism, most ingenious and innovative ideas would have been neglected or passed over simply because they were against the social norms.

As we learn from history, anything remotely innovative or out of the box has been shunned by society at large. Most individuals consider innovation to be a direct attack on their way of life, while others perceive inventions and state-of-the-art ideas to be a complete waste of time. However, a capitalistic society believes in the innovator and gives them the funds necessary to realize their ambitions. A capitalist allows the youth to work on their business purpose and transform it into a cultural phenomenon. Conversely, if we were to take the case of a neoliberalist or socialist society, the young entrepreneur would never get the opportunity to turn their aspirations into a reality. This is mainly because socialism breeds a system that relies on extensive government involvement with little to no individual freedom.

In a socialist state, no matter how ingenious the idea may be, it needs to go through a lengthy screening process by several government authorities. If it does not go through these channels, the idea will not be entertained and probably never see the light of day. Even if the idea has the solution to most of the nation's problems, it could be overlooked in a socialist or neoliberal state.

On the contrary, in a capitalist framework, every business solution or idea is given a chance to prove its merit. Instead of conclusively undermining the idea, the capitalist system allows it to grow and make a mark in the industry. Through the free market system, nearly every investor, entrepreneur, or business professional can choose to enter the industry and establish their brand or product line. All they need to do is create a product or service that effectively meets the demands of the marketplace. If the entrepreneur succeeds in creating or meeting the demands, they can rest assured that their brand will reach the very peaks of the market or industry. However, by chance, if the entrepreneur fails to meet the demands of the consumer base and is unable to develop a niche market for their product line, they will not be successful in their respective industry. In other words, we can say that the success or failure of an individual or business ultimately depends on their efforts and innovation.

There is no external party dictating the entrepreneur's future in capitalism. On the other hand, the entrepreneur has the freedom to operate as they wish, wherever they wish, and when they wish. Considering the ideals of the free market, the entreprencurs are given a free hand and expected to give their best. Moreover, because of this, young entrepreneurs do everything in their power to meet their client's expectations. For them, nothing matters more than living up to the customer's expectations. Consequently, these young entrepreneurs bring out even more innovative, state-of-the-art, and useful products for their consumer base. This is the power of the free market and capitalism, and the sooner people realize this, they can bring immense ease and comfort in their personal and professional life. Preferably, the youth of America needs to understand that capitalism is fundamentally advanced. The tenets of capitalism are not futuristic by choice. On the other hand, the very structure of a capitalistic society paves the way for societal growth on all levels. This is mainly because the attributes that reinforce market economies, which include the likes of investment, accumulation, carry an underlying idea.

The idea is that eventually, the economy at large will grow considerably, maybe not today but somewhere in the near future. This belief is present in a capitalistic society and cannot be taken away from the average citizen. In addition to this, the free market system is, in most cases, not concerned with how the product came to be or what is the brand's motive. Instead, the participants of the free market system are only concerned with, "what's new?"

If entrepreneurs can bring innovation, they can surely succeed in any industry. Although if they keep on relying on old patterns and do not pay any attention to innovation, they will never be able to sustain themselves and will always fall short of expectations. This fact alone makes capitalism the most equality-based socioeconomic system in the known world. What's more, because of capitalism's future orientation, it can be hailed as the striking hallmark of modernity. It is important to note that ordinarily, pre-capitalist societies relied a lot on the past. They were too dependent on myths, old religions, and ancestral lines and considered them to be the only methods of existence. However, their assumption and the system itself couldn't be more flawed. We have clearly seen that past economic, political, and social structures cannot successfully be applied in the modern-day. The reason behind this is that the problems, advantages, structure, routines, and other conveniences will not survive in the modern age.

The society was completely different in the past, with separate values, instincts, and the enthusiasm to live. So, the digital age youth has no choice but to look forward and seek answers to their own problems. Fortunately, capitalist societies always look to the future. They don't rely on outdated systems, technologies, and determinations to ensure their future. On the contrary, the capitalistic system relies on inventions, broader horizons, and far greater abundance. *"Oh, the places you will go!"* is the defining text of market capitalism. To understand capitalism, we must also understand that chance is a mixed blessing. Opportunity and uncertainty go hand in hand. Critics of capitalism often point out that it leads to an uncertain future. However, this is not the case. Economic growth ultimately requires change and disruption. To understand this, we can see that Schumpeter's *"creative destruction"* could possibly impose some immediate social costs. However, no one can ever predict or know where market dynamics will lead us. Nobody in the world could have predicted Facebook and Twitter. However, this assumption is false for the overall picture. If the economy grows at a rapid pace, considering market capitalism, we can easily predict with confidence that the future will be better than the present.

All in all, capitalism has kept this promise quite well throughout history. If we were to compare with earlier periods, the material conditions of life have improved phenomenally since the birth of capitalism. In the last 500 years, up to around 1700, economic output per person was flat. We can also say that the average person in the 1700s was no better off, economically speaking, than the average person in the 1200s. These values are given as per the calculations done by The World in Data, led by Max Roser. Moreover, they make this point both visually and dramatically clear. Overall, the natural idea of economic improvement is now so culturally embedded that even half a decade of no progress causes alarm bells to ring, let alone half a millennium ago.

"The past is another country" is the opening line of LP Hartley's 1953 novel, The Go-Between. *"They do things differently there."* We can easily claim that Hartley's perspective is another deeply modern thought, which is now an uncontroversial sentiment. In previous eras, the past was entirely the same country, at least in economic terms. This is because these countries did everything pretty much the same as in the past. In a feudal or agricultural economy, things in the modern-day are likely to be quite similar to things a century ago, as well as to the developments a century later.

Once the capitalism engine accelerated, the future entered our collective imagination. In fact, novels began to be set there. The term "science fiction" was born. In practical terms, economic forecasting and prediction became an industry. Most people ask, what will the U.S. economy be like in 2030, or 2050? How big? What jobs will it contain? How many? A great deal of time and resources are spent, both by governments and companies, simply attempting to answer these pressing questions, as efficiently as they can. In the case of more than 99% of human history, a belief that life is going to get better – on earth, not just in heaven – would have been considered eccentric for some. They would think things like, "maybe my children would have more than me; maybe not." In either scenario, the condition of the future was unlikely to have much to do with human activities. Therefore, pre-capitalist societies tended to be extremely religious. In their mind, a good harvest was in the hands of weather systems, which implied that it was in the hands of the gods.

If the promise of a better future starts to fade, a vicious cycle sets in. Why save? Why sacrifice? Why stick to education for longer? Marx accused religion of being the opium of the masses, thus distracting them from capitalist exploitation. However, capitalism has steadily undermined superstition by proving to be more promising. It did this by promising that the future will, in fact, be materially better as a result of the manmade market. Although putting most promises aside, perhaps the greatest promise of capitalism is that each generation will ride on the shoulders of the one before. They will do this mainly because of the natural workings of a market economy. It should be no surprise in anyone's mind that the greatest issues to capitalism come when that promise begins to be questioned. If capitalism loses its leash on the future generation or the youth, it will be in trouble. Therefore, the youth needs to embrace capitalism and avail its advantages as much as possible.

It is important to note one crucial fact that markets run on primarily- one thing, psychology. We work to live. However, we also work with a reasonable hope that it will enable us to live better in the future. This is done by getting more rewards out of the market as we grow in experience and skill. In addition to this, the goal can be accomplished by saving and so, through what Keynes described as the *"magic"* of compound interest. This magic, in turn, benefits immensely from general economic progress. At an individual level, we might even claim that we are saving for a rainy day. Although together, savings greatly propitiate capital accumulation for investment, which substantially increases growth and prosperity. As a result of these steps, we may even look forward in our later years to another modern invention: a *"lucrative retirement."* In the end, no one argues that economic progress ultimately spans across the generations. This is because parents normally envision their children's standard of living to surpass their own eventually. At the same time, the children in question expect their offspring to continue the history and become better than them. It is our fundamental human instinct to see our children flourish. And this instinct has been powerfully channeled through market-led growth.

We work not only for ourselves but for the imminent future of our children. Therefore, we choose to invest in their education so that their enhanced skills will mean a better life for them and their families. As a result, people will be only willing to invest in a better future if, and it is an extremely big if, there is a potential chance that it will pay off. Moreover, they will also invent if the concerned system consistently brings them a better future. Capitalism not only produces a society focused on the future, but it also needs it. If the promise of a better future starts to fade, a vicious cycle will inevitably set in. Then, people will begin asking questions such as, why save? Why sacrifice? Or, why stick at education for a longer duration? Plus, if more and more doubt creeps in, people will tend to perform less, learn less, and save less. This will, in turn, cause growth to be slow, thereby fulfilling their own misguided prophecies. Hence, the biggest threat to capitalism is socialism, and if it is not subdued, it will cause immense havoc on American society. Again, we need to understand that Capitalism is intrinsically growth-oriented and built upon this reality. We need to understand that capital markets don't work well in a stationary state. On the contrary, they are reminiscent of sharks, either moving or dead.

Nobody has ever satisfactorily described a no-growth, market-based model. At the same time, the entrepreneur should know that only the best thinkers decide that enough is enough. In actual fact, the vast majority of their fellow citizens, who look up at them, might actually feel different and be willing to avail the promises of capitalism.[7] Based on these realities, we can easily say that capitalism has a lot to offer to the nation's youth. It is high time people start realizing this fact before the opportunity escapes. They need to rely on the current system and try to avail the benefits as much as possible. Rather than paying attention to the myths

---

[7] Reeves (2019), Capitalism used to promise a better future. Can it still do that? Retrieved
from https://www.theguardian.com/commentisfree/2019/may/22/capitalism-broken-better-future-can-it-do-that

and lies of society, the youth of this nation needs to focus on the surface and make the best of their freedom. Moreover, the youth needs to understand the implications of socialism and what effects it will have on American society. They must comprehend the dangers of socialism and how lethal this system could prove to be in the near future. Once they do this, the nation's youth will finally be able to improve their lives and avail the promise that has been guaranteed to them.

Chapter 17
The Dangers of Socialism to the Youth

"Socialism is a philosophy of failure, the creed of ignorance, and the gospel of envy, its inherent virtue is the equal sharing of misery."

–Winston Churchill

We have already gained an understanding of the various advantages of capitalism and how this immaculate sociopolitical system can benefit the youth of America. Now, we will focus on the very real threat of socialism and why today's generation needs to reject this ideology once and for all. In recent times, we have somewhat seen an inclination towards socialism by the young people of America. And, this phenomenon must be a major concern for liberty-loving Americans. This is mainly because socialism limits the true potential of the young population. No matter how talented and ingenious the person maybe, in a socialist society, their dreams and ambitions will never come to fruition. Unlike the notion of equality preached by leftists and socialist propagandists, the promise of a socialist nation is quite different. The average citizen's efforts and sacrifice only benefit a few people at the top. The ruling party or government receives all the benefits of the common man's hard labor. And, because of this, the person never gets an opportunity to grow and receive their worth. All the while, the socialist government reinforces the illusion of equality. This is the true *promise* of socialism, and the sooner the youth realizes it, the better chances they will have of securing a prosperous future for themselves and their families.

This is one of the many reasons why President Donald Trump has made a promise to the American people that this precious country will never become a socialist nation. He is aware of the dangers of socialism to the common man and knows that the only way to succeed is in the path of our forefathers. The United States was built on the foundations of capitalism for one crucial reason. This vital reason was that our Founding Fathers believed that every person has the right to earn and live according to their own wishes. They believed in **true equality** and ensured that each individual was allowed to elevate his/her worth, progress, and social standing. Considering the horrors of socialism, most conservative politicians and media gurus agree with Trump's ideas and are willing to support him through any means necessary. However, it is safe to say that only ridiculing socialist ideas and counting on America always to remain a federal republic is simply not enough to combat socialism. On the contrary, the government and its machinery need to enlighten the common man regarding the implications of socialism. What's more, this educational campaign must be directed towards the nation's youth so they can become aware of this decadent system and withdraw their support immediately.

It is important to note that the major cause of socialism's upsurge is none other than the leftists' proficiency in controlling the narrative. While this may be a difficult fact to face, it is a reality that needs to be addressed as soon as possible. In actuality, the left has a tight grip on public education, the news media along, and the entertainment industry of the nation. And, for the last two generations, the leftists controlling these mediums have, unfortunately, changed the opinions of what America is to millions of young people. Because their propaganda has reached a point of critical mass, these underhanded individuals are looking to compel the same young people to cast aside our impeccable republic in favor of a socialist regime. If God forbid this regime ever takes a foothold in the United States, the country will, in effect, lose its liberty. The American youth need to see past the illusions and façade created by the leftists and come to terms with reality. They need to understand how detrimental socialism is to the wellbeing of every person in the known world. What's more, the young generation needs to acquaint themselves with institutions that show socialism's real picture.

Just recently, a brand-new organization has stepped into the American social structure to combat these underhanded schemers and propagandists. This organization is none other than the Young Americans Against Socialism (YAAS), and its primary objective is spreading the factual implications of a socialist structure. They can accomplish this feat by sharing true stories of the young people who had to suffer at the hands of a socialist government. Morgan Zegers originally founded this group. Morgan Zegers is the 22-year-old daughter of an Iraq War veteran, and she even ran for the New York State Assembly in 2018. She did this mainly to prevent the downward economic spiral of her home state. Over the years, Morgan Zegers had received a lot of media attention for her, unfortunately, failed effort. Still, Miss Zegers was crowned as a Rising Star of the New York G.O.P. and the New York Young Republicans. According to Zeger, socialism needs to be curbed before it takes root in our great country. To accomplish this feat, Zegers's ingenious strategy is utilizing two of the left's powerful tools against them. These two tools are none other than emotion and social media. In Zeger's mind, social media is the most obvious place to have these kinds of important conversations.

This is mainly because this is where Zegers believes that she will find her audience and convince them accordingly. As per Zegers, the main reason why socialists depend on emotion is that it produces swift and powerful responses. In addition to this, Zegers also states that emotion ends up clouding basic reason and judgment. And, she believes that these two fundamental concepts are Kryptonite to any socialist idea. Thankfully, the videos YAAS has posted on social media have the emotional stories of young people who have directly been impacted under socialism and have blessedly escaped this mafia's control. The youth is free to watch them and become enlightened on this decadent system.Putting aside the videos, Zegers will also utilize the platform of social media to set the record straight about socialism. Among the many myths which will be dispelled in the long haul is the so-called heroism of the prolific murderer Che Guevara, along with how the left constantly persists on wrongly classifying Scandinavian countries as socialist. The reality and the aftermath of the oil-rich Venezuela.

Finally, how the immaculate machinery of capitalism has taken more people out of poverty than any other economic system in known history, in light of her youth and her immensely dedicated social media strategy, Zegers is in a far better position to alter the narrative of the youth. There is no doubting the fact that Zegers will fare way better than a typical news anchor that most young people probably won't even watch. In all honesty, it is refreshing and exciting to see another group dedicated to pushing back against socialism's appeal to America's youth. As a matter of fact, it has been a long time coming, and as Zegers contends, we, as a nation, need to corner socialism as civil liberty, and that it is worth fighting for.[8] Aside from Zegers and the YAAS, there is a plethora of politicians, diplomats, and thinkers that are openly debunking these lies. In fact, a resident politician considers socialism to be a direct attack on the American people's values. They claimed that most of the young generation do not seem to understand the ramifications of socialism. The resident politician says that apparently, there is a clear misunderstanding regarding what socialism is and what it represents.

Based on the propaganda circulated in major media platforms, a considerable number of our young people *believe* that socialism is a solution to the ills and misconducts of society. Some think of it as a cult of personality and believe that they will be viewed as enigmas of society by joining its ranks. However, the youth's lack of knowledge and misunderstanding of facts could be a devastating blow for the country. As a matter of fact, this blow could be so severe that this great nation may never recover from it.

---

[8] Morris (2019), Educating Youth on the Dangers of Socialism. Retrieved from https://patriotpost.us/articles/64928-educating-youth-on-the-dangers-of-socialism-2019-08-20

So, naturally, one vital question comes to the mind of any sane and logical American. This pressing question is that how is it even possible for socialism to receive even this much attention? According to the resident politician, the answer is that there is a great disconnect between the people and the inherent realities of the world's socioeconomic structure. As an example, we can observe the results of the Rasmussen poll that was conducted just after the 2018 midterm elections.

According to the Rasmussen poll, nearly 40 percent of millennials loved socialism. Although upon conducting further evaluation, it was discovered by the organization that 60 percent of millennials that loved socialism also believed the government must be *less* involved in their business. There are multiple reasons for this misconception. However, perhaps the most obvious cause must be none other than the word "socialism" and our method of hearing it. He further adds socialism's meaning in the American vernacular has been altered significantly. He further adds that this change has probably altered American youth's perception of the world's most heinous criminals. Based on the results of the survey, the politician wonders whether or not millennials are aware that Hitler was a socialist. This is mainly because the very word 'Nazi' was originally taken from the term 'National Socialist.' Nazi's staunch ally Mussolini was a known fascist. If we were to look at the definition of fascism, it is, in fact, the total control of industry by the nation's government! Moreover, the definition of socialist is also synonymous with the ownership of industry by the government.

Does the youth see much of a difference? The politician doesn't seem to believe so. Because, according to him, when words become co-opted and abused, all true meaning is lost. Karl Marx is viewed by many as the father of modern socialism. In his book *"The Communist Manifesto,"* he stated that through socialism, there would be a gradual *"withering away"* of government completely.

He literally called it the withering away of the state. In practice, though, socialism makes the government far bigger and more powerful. What's more, the people of the nation are the ones who, in actuality, wither away. The resident politician is a Venezuelan immigrant, and he has personally experienced the withering of his home and brethren. He truly knows, more than most, what the false promises of socialism mean for the average citizen, particularly those people who lack sufficient resources. They are the people who are most exposed and will tend to become enticed by these false promises. Venezuela was, at a time, the most prosperous nation in Latin America. In fact, it was the fourth wealthiest in the world, and then Venezuela voted for socialism. According to the politician, the period between his coming to America as a child and officially becoming a U.S. citizen in 2004. He sadly witnessed from afar how the nation went from bad to worse. The nation became so decadent that it was reduced to bread lines and bank runs in a span of only 22 years.

As an American, the politician is deeply concerned about the future of America. This is mainly because he feels that corrupt promises tempt the youth. In his mind, Americans must concentrate on what made this nation prosperous and free. It was certainly not free stuff. It's the Bill of Rights, along with the American people's hard work and ingenuity. He also adds that terms like *"democratic socialism"* are just oxymorons masking the true danger of socialism. He feels that the American people can vote their way into socialism, but they need to fight their way out. This is simply because socialism needs big government to operate. Once the people transfer their power to the government, it is next to impossible to take it back. By doing this, the people would have successfully created an all-powerful one percent that will rule over us with an iron fist. [9] The irony here is that even American *"socialists"* possibly don't support government ownership of production. This is mainly because whenever people ask self-proclaimed socialists what they want, these individuals mostly give vague and weird answers.

According to Ocasio-Cortez, *"In a modern, moral and wealthy society, no person in America should be too poor to live."* Moreover, in the Liza Minnelli musical, *Flora the Red Menace*, the communist organizer actually sings, *"Are you in favor of democracy, the rights of man, everlasting peace, milk and cookies for the kids, security, jobs for everyone, and against slums, the filthy rich, and making cannon fodder of our youth? Then you're a communist!"*

---

[9]Rucker (2019), Young People Misunderstand Socialism and Its Effects. Retrieved from https://www.washingtontimes.com/news/2019/oct/30/young-people-misunderstand-socialism-and-its-effec/

Any pragmatic and mentally stable person can see the contradictions. One of the main advocates of socialism, Sanders, has pointed to Denmark as a classic example of democratic socialism. However, the Danes deny this statement categorically. This is mainly because, in 2015, the Danish prime minister went on to state, *"Some people in the U.S. associate the Nordic model with some sort of socialism. I would like to make one thing clear. Denmark is far from a socialist planned economy. Denmark is a market economy."* If Denmark is the so-called model for modern-day American socialists, then they should effectively leave the D.S.A. and officially join Democrats for Higher Taxes and Transfer Payments.

Furthermore, an in-depth analysis of Gallup's latest poll points to a clear lack of interest in the form of government control that socialism would entail. The participants were asked if they had a positive or negative image of various things. And, these respondents had given mostly high marks to small business, entrepreneurship, and free enterprise. What's more, the same participants had a 56 percent approval for capitalism. In addition to this, the federal government and socialism lagged far behind by 39 and 37 percent, respectively. These are the actual responses for all respondents and not just young people. Out of these respondents, only 44 percent had agreed that *"government should do more to solve our country's problems."* All the while, 25 percent claimed that there is too little government regulation of business. At the same time, 39 percent said it was too much, and 33 percent stated that it was the right amount. Apart from this, a 2017 Gallup study highlighted that 67 percent of Americans argued that big government was a far graver threat to the future than huge corporations.

Also, 26 percent of the participants had picked big business, while 5 percent stated that big labor was a big issue. If socialism stands for anything, it stands for giving more power to the government. However, almost no one in the new Gallup poll believes that the federal government has too little power. Only 8 percent in the new poll think that the government has no control ever since 2002. Looking at the present situation, there is widespread debate in the United States about how high taxes and spending ought to be. We know that Americans like free enterprise, and very few of them will EVER opt for a more powerful government.[10]

---

[10]Boaz (2018), Young People like 'Socialism,' but Do They Know What it is?

Furthermore, after understanding the core nature of socialism, it is high time for the American youth to destroy any and all illusions regarding this failed system. The nation's youth needs to strengthen the capitalist structure of the country and reap the true and ample benefits of their labor and steer the nation toward everlasting progress, just like the many generations before them!

[1]Boaz (2018), Young People like 'Socialism,' but Do They Know What it is? Retrieved from https://www.cato.org/publications/commentary/young-people-socialism-do-they-know-what-it-is

---

Retrieved from https://www.cato.org/publications/commentary/young-people-socialism-do-they-know-what-it

Chapter 18
No nation has ever thrived under Socialism

"The function of socialism is to raise suffering to a higher level."

–Normal Mailer

After understanding the many dangers of socialism and how these perils can affect the American youth, we will now expose the realities of socialism and how this system has ruined the countries that practiced it. In view of the new surge of enthusiasm towards socialism, the American people need to understand how this socioeconomic system has impacted the nations of its birth and those that embraced it. If we were to delve deeper into history, we would discover that socialism has brought nothing but utter misery and ruin to every country where it has been practiced. No country has been spared the fate of utter socioeconomic collapse. Before long, former superpowers turned into a miserable shadow of what they were. We can find numerous examples of socialism's failure throughout the world.

However, despite this, some Americans are leaning towards the *"socialist"* banner. For these ill-informed individuals, socialism is a new and exciting system. However, in actuality, this socioeconomic system is anything but new. On the contrary, this specific political vision has been tried numerous times, in many situations, and a plethora of places. And, if we were to evaluate the results, they would represent a long list of failures. We can assess the most recent failure of socialism, Venezuela.

During the late 1990s, when Hugo Chavez rose to power, he immediately communicated an ambiguously driven *"revolution"* that was *"anti-Yanqui."* This implied that the new government in Venezuela would be pro-Cuba and take special care of the poor and the needy. What's more, Chavez had planned and implemented government intervention in the Venezuelan economy. This intervention resulted in a dramatic increase in spending on social programs. Also, this increase was multiplied and sustained through seemingly limitless oil revenues. During his tenure, Chavez had been successful in four national elections in a row. However, the economy witnessed considerable shortages in necessities. This occurred primarily because oil prices fell sharply under the regime of Chavez's hand-picked successor, Nicolas Maduro. And through Maduro's reign, the Venezuelan people and the rest of the world gained awareness on the vital flaw in *"Chavismo."* Under Maduro, the inflation in Venezuela rose to a staggering 1 million percent, and the country's poverty rate went past 80 percent. Considering these unfortunate circumstances, the vast majority of Venezuelans had no choice but to go to bed hungry.

What's more, the country's electrical power began shrinking, medicine became scarce, and a once booming Latin American country was dramatically turned into a failed state. Over 15 percent of the population had to flee from the country because of this socioeconomic collapse. This massive exodus from Venezuela has even contributed to the refugee situation in Syria.

Surprisingly enough, the circumstances and demise of Venezuela is only the recent example of the story a generation of young Americans desperately need to hear. The narrative of socialism originally began well over two centuries ago. The word *"socialism"* was coined in the 1820s by the adherents of British and French visionaries. Some of these so-called visionaries include Robert Owen and Charles Fourier. These individuals were the first to create experimental communes. These communes were mostly found on the American soil. What's more, these people wished to live lives on the fundamentals of sharing and equality. Moreover, these individuals honestly believed that life would be ecstatic and more harmonious because of these communes. In their mind, these individuals believed that their example would compel the rest of the world that they had found a new and better method of surviving.

Both Fourier and Owen managed to create a total of 40 to 50 such communes. Nearly each of them horribly met their end. Figuratively, the average lifespan of these communes was a meager two years. The main reason behind the failure of these communes was well-documented. It was managed through the surviving correspondence from the most celebrated socialist commune located in New Harmony in Indiana. The commune's member highlighted that *"The gardens and fields were almost entirely neglected."* While another member pointed out that *"There has been much irregularity of effort."* Meanwhile, the third member reported that *"Instead of striving who should do most, the most industry was manifested in accusing others of doing little.*" Despite this failed start, socialism somehow managed to survive, particularly through the rhetorical powers of Karl Marx and Friedrich Engels. These two individuals would go on to suspend communal experiments as *"utopian."* They pointed out that, because of socialism, they had discovered *"scientific socialism."* This philosophy, much like other socialist agendas, was met with inevitable opposition by the public who feared that they would turn complete societies to socialism. However, the people who were inspired by this vision were not prepared for the eventuality of this failed system. Before long, Lenin seized power in Russia in 1917.

This rise to power effectively launched the world's next big attempt at socialism. Considering Lenin's dictatorial ideology, more than fourteen nearby nations were brought into what became the new Union of Soviet Socialist Republics. Then, with time, more than 17 other countries officially came under the banner of communism. It is important to note that the efforts used to implement socialism by force had caused the deaths of tens of millions of lives. Lenin had created a police state characterized by the *"Gulag Archipelago."* This dogmatic politician failed to create even a shred of prosperity or happiness. In the modern-day, out of the 32 countries that became the *"Communist bloc"* during the Cold War, little over six such regimes remained intact. Of these countries, the largest nation, China, is adhering to the type of crony capitalism under authoritarian rule in the present rule. The socialist adherents who had forbidden Lenin's autocratic ways went on to create *"democratic socialism."* They did this because they also wanted to abolish capitalism in favor of *"common ownership of the means of production, distribution, and exchange."* This statement was put forward by the British Labor Party's charter. However, these individuals wished their ideology to be implemented peacefully and constitutionally. They wanted their agenda to be fulfilled by winning elections and offering a legislative change.

Decades following World War II, these parties, which were often called Socialist, Labor, or Social Democratic, would win elections across western Europe and in a couple of other areas. Unsurprisingly, they experienced the same failures as their predecessors. They would improve social safety nets, initiate fresh business regulations, and even help labor unions. However, when they started socializing the *"means of production,"* the results were extremely disastrous. It had worsened to such an extent that these individuals had to relinquish this project or were voted out. Then, in the 1980s, just a year following the French Socialist Party rise to power, the same party had vouched for the "rupture" of capitalism. This is mainly because the general secretary advocated the need for *"bringing about a real reconciliation between the left and the economy."* In summary, these socialist parties had figured out that they could reform capitalism by taxing away some of the wealth created in the private sector for public purposes. Yet still, these parties could never, in any way, develop a socialist state.

In addition, during the post-war period, several new nations had emerged out of Europe's former colonial empires. This was encouraged by both the United Nations and Western development experts. What's more, these parties had even embraced *"African or Arab socialism."* This system was promoted as a way for developing countries to catch up. Moreover, this surge had paved the way for forced-paced development through central *"planning."* In this planning, the government had to compute the country's basic needs, including roads, electricity, and potable water.

Then, after computing these needs, the government had to summon the necessary actions. The result of these actions led to a couple of decades of stunted growth. This lack of growth continued up until their Western advisors had comprehended the contrary involvement of the so-called *"Four Tigers"* of East Asia, namely Taiwan, South Korea, Singapore, and Hong Kong. All these countries were rising from poverty by promoting private investment and shipping goods for export. Following their example, the developing countries had moved away from socialism completely. After this, the global rates of poverty were reduced significantly.

In totality, for well over two centuries, socialism had been implemented in nearly every corner of the planet. All the varieties that socialism adherents could conjure up, none of these systems have prevailed in the country. Young people can point out that they were never taught any of this in history. But, how can we justify the struggles of modern-day socialists and neoliberals? We can't as these individuals are blinded by ideology since they regularly find something of value in one of the most vicious socialist dictatorships. These socialists only look at dictatorships' achievements, such as Fidel Castro's literacy programs or the Soviet Union's subway system.[11] In any case, these politicians need to be ignored at all costs if we, the American people, want true prosperity in the country.

There is no doubting the fact that socialism is the biggest lie of the twentieth century. On the surface, it may have promised prosperity, equality, and security. However, it had delivered poverty, misery, and tyranny. On the contrary, equality was accomplished only in the sense that everyone was equal in his or her misery.

This is the same scenario in which a Ponzi scheme or chain letter initially prospers but ultimately collapses. It has been experienced that socialism may show early signs of success. However, any accomplishments swiftly transform into fundamental deficiencies of central planning. It is, in fact, the illusion of success that enables the government to intervene with its malicious and vindictive appeal. In the long haul, socialism will always remain a formula for tyranny and misery.

---

[11] Muravchik & Walworth (2020), Sanders Camp Ignores Socialism's Total Failure. Retrieved from https://www.realclearpolitics.com/articles/2020/03/03/sanders_camp_ignores_s ocialisms_total_failure.html

This is mainly because a pyramid structure is inevitably unmanageable. This transpires because the system is dependent on faulty and irregular principles. Similarly, collectivism is unmanageable in the long run because it is nothing but a detrimental theory. Socialism simply doesn't work as it is not consistent with the basic principles of human behavior. The utter failure of socialism in countries can be linked to one vital defect. This defect is none other than the fact that the system completely negates incentives.

On the contrary, in a capitalist economy, incentives are of universal significance. This is mainly because, principles like prices, the profit-and-loss system of accounting, and private property rights offer an efficient, interrelated system of incentives. These systems manage to guide and influence economic behavior.

Capitalism is dependent on the theory that incentives matter! However, under socialism, incentives can either play a negligible role or are ignored completely. A centrally planned economy that is not dependent on market prices or profits, where the state owns the property, is nothing but a system that has no effective incentive mechanism to control economic activity. By failing to stress on incentives, socialism is by default in direct contradiction with human nature and is hence doomed to fail. We can even say that socialism is based on the theory that incentives don't matter! However, the strength of capitalism can be linked to an incentive structure revolving around the three Ps:

1. Prices determined by market forces,
2. A profit-and-loss system of accounting
3. Private property rights.

The failure of socialism can be largely seen through the sheer neglect of these three incentive-promoting components. As a result of their failure to foster, promote, and nurture their people's potential, these centrally controlled economies deprive the human spirit of fulfillment. What's more, socialism fails utterly because it kills and destroys the human spirit.

If people have any doubts about this matter, they can look at the examples of people leaving Cuba in homemade rafts and boats. Or, those individuals who are in long lines in Venezuela struggling, and often failing to procure food and some even have to comb through garbage bins in search of food remnants. The Delilah of socialism is consistently luring us with the offer: *"Give up a little of your freedom, and I will give you a little more security."* However, as the experience of this century has demonstrated, the bargain is tempting, but it never pays off. This is mainly because, we, the people, end up losing both our freedom and our security.

Socialism will remain a constant temptation for the ignorant and dimwitted. Therefore, we must be vigilant in our fight against socialism, not only around the world but also here in the United States. The failure of socialism had propagated a worldwide renaissance of freedom and liberty. For the first time in history, the day is finally coming when a plethora of people will live in free societies, and societies are constantly moving towards freedom.

Capitalism will play a conclusive and major role in the global revival of liberty and prosperity. This is mainly because, this ideal system fosters the human spirit, stimulates human creativity, and encourages the spirit of enterprise. Just by creating a powerful system of incentives that promotes thrift, hard work, and efficiency, capitalism creates exceptional wealth. And, the main difference between capitalism and socialism is that capitalism works.[12]

---

[12] Perry (2016), Why Socialism always fails. Retrieved from https://www.aei.org/carpe-diem/why-socialism-always-fails/

In fact, two quite different pieces of news point out the unquestionable failure of socialism. They focus on the cruel repression by Venezuelan President Nicolás Maduro and the unsurprising result of the French elections. Venezuelan socialism, as mentioned previously, is nothing but a self-deprecating expression of extreme socialist ideas. This is the form of Marxism that, when applied for the first time in Russia just 100 years ago, was referred to as communism.

On the contrary, like most Europeans, the French showed that they no longer have faith in the other variant of socialism. This is the so-called "light" or moderate form that has been named social democracy or democratic socialism in many nations.

Both ideologies agree on a fundamental point. This point is none other than the rejection of capitalism and the free market economy. This immaculate system offers everyone the right to produce and consume according to their needs and desires. However, socialists wish to eliminate it completely. On the other hand, the rest wish to control it and lessen it to its minimum expression. Venezuelan socialists have shown that they have the same oppressive calling as their Soviet and Chinese predecessors, along with their

Cuban counterparts. These socialists not only sunk a rich oil nation into poverty but have also shown that their alleged democracy is nothing but a farce. This is mainly because these individuals do not waver in brutally repressing their people when they protest.

At the same time, the Venezuelan dictatorship's continuous aggression toward private property has developed an economy incapable of sustaining or providing the goods that people need. Scarcity, inflation, and unemployment are the immediate consequences of this way of governing.

What's more, it leads to dictatorship and repression, especially of citizens who try to rise against it. As a result of this totalitarian form of understanding socialism, a different, democratic, and less extreme version of it has grown in Europe and the United States. For decades, Social Democrats have been a major political party in Europe and have shaped the societies of almost all their countries. All the while, in the United States, the Democratic Party has been endorsing and applying similar policies since the 1930s. However, now the political landscape has changed drastically. The Socialist Party of France managed to earn only 6.2% of the vote and so achieved fifth place. All the while, English Labor Party supporters are experiencing an internal crisis of deep character. What's more, the Spanish socialists are struggling to sustain second place, and a similar situation is going on in Germany and Scandinavia. Parties of the populist right, extreme left, and even some liberals are going against socialism. The left has done horribly in the recent free elections carried out in Latin America, and there are no signs of greater influence in Asia or Africa.

Socialists developed a model of government that, based on exceedingly high taxes, was originally intended to transfer the wealth of those who have a lot to those who have the least. They tried to accomplish this by developing the so-called welfare state, in which health, education, pensions, and sometimes even housing became benefits provided by the government. Markets were regulated in various ways, and controls were imposed on production. This model of government prevails today in Europe, but such intervention in society reveals its limitations over time. The size and expenditure of governments have been increasing, thereby resulting in colossal debt and severe economic woes. These systems have been increasingly ineffective in offering the services they promise to provide, so they weaken the rights and values of a free society. Therefore, people should not be naïve and think that today's voters don't know that the welfare state is a failed experiment. The discomfort is obvious, especially when considering the implications of huge, unproductive, and exploitive governments. It explains why moderate socialists are encountering heavy losses in elections across the world.

It's safe to say the only fundamental solution is to convalesce individual freedoms, accept the need for a free economy, and considerably diminish the state's functions and extent. This needs to be done not only in Europe but all over the known world.[13] As soon as the American people understand this reality, they will finally be in a position to right their wrongs and propel our country into a new era of growth and progress. All the youth needs to do is take out the time to learn about the true nature of socialism. They should not believe what their left-leaning professors tell them but do independent research in books, journals, and the internet and videos to discover the dangers of the socialist

---

[13] Sabino (2017), From Venezuela to France, Socialism is Failing all over the World. Retrieved from https://panampost.com/carlos-sabino/2017/04/27/socialism-is-failing-all-over-the-world/?cn-reloaded=1

ideology and the devastations it has always left in its paths. Just by doing this, they will figure out what future lies ahead for our great country if, God forbid, it is taken over by a socialist agenda. By knowing this truth, the American youth will automatically strengthen the capitalistic core of the country and gain immensely in the long haul. Moreover, these independent studies will expose socialism for what it truly is.

Chapter 19
The Real Threat
Communism/Socialism
Poses to the Religious
World

"The fact that free men persist in search for the truth is the essential difference between Communism and Democracy."

–Robert Kennedy

By now, we have gained awareness of the frail and disastrous promise of socialism/communism and how this ideology has ruined the lives of millions of people. However, we failed to address the very real threat communist and socialist regimes pose for world religions. This chapter will focus on this threat and expose just how serious this threat is to the spiritual and religious community. Looking back in history, we come to notice that communism and socialism have always persecuted religious people and institutions.

This is mainly because, as per the communist or socialist ideology, religion has no significance in the sociopolitical existence of any individual. In fact, the early pioneers of socialism and communism, such as Karl Marx, have openly criticized religion in their literary and verbal communications. Because of this propaganda, communist and socialist nations have made it their vendetta to annihilate religions and their followers from the map. These countries have feared religions to such an extent that religious persecution, in most countries, became a part of their constitutions and social structures. Religious leaders and followers were not only prevented from exercising their basic rights, but were also tortured, jailed, and brutally killed for their belief in many cases.

A classic example of this would be Soviet Russia and the horrors committed by the regime after World War II. Under the leadership of dictators like Stalin and Lenin, the communist regime had forced its way into every household in the Soviet Union, and the whole nation was under strict surveillance. This surveillance was carried out by secret agencies of the Kremlin like the K.G.B. and other factions of the secret police. These agencies carried out perhaps the most vicious human rights violations in human history. While many socialist and communist enthusiasts might argue that the violations came as a direct result of dictatorships, the position and policies of these regimes have not changed even in the modern-day.

Socialist and communist countries are still carrying out the same persecutions on the major religions of the world and are not willing to tolerate and provide the most fundamental human rights. To make matters worse, quite recently, a certain country has started to use its people's social and financial conditions to turn them away from their faith and belief systems. This country is the self-proclaimed new superpower of the world and has rapidly improved its socioeconomic situation in recent years. The country is none other than communist China, and it has taken the war against religion to an entirely new low.

As per the findings of the *South China Morning Post* (SCMP) in 2017, the Communist Party of China or (C.P.C.) representatives had secretly visited the homes of believers in Yugan county of Jiangxi province. This province has over 10% Christians, and in this visit, the officials forced the residents to replace the photos of the

Lord Jesus Christ with posters of President Xi Jinping. The intrusion led to the removal of more than 600 Christian symbols from living rooms. These symbols were then replaced by 453 portraits of the communist leader. Upon further investigation, the report stated that this action was an element of a government campaign to lessen poverty in the region. This was mainly because, according to C.P.C. members, Christian believers' faith was the main cause of their family's financial miseries and woes.

We can easily see that these forced replacements in villagers' homes highlight the fact that the party wants its people to view the leaders of China as their saviors. When the local Chinese paper contacted the campaign leader, he said, *"Many poor households have plunged into poverty because of illness in the family. Some resorted to believing in Jesus to cure their illnesses."*

The campaign leader added, *"We tried to tell them that getting ill is a physical thing and that the people who can really help them are the Communist Party and General Secretary Xi."* Moreover, some Christians in Yugan County voiced their concern that they would not receive any government aid if they didn't comply with the campaigners' wishes. In other words, if the average Christian home viewed General Secretary Xi Jinping as their lord and savior, the family would immediately come out of the shackles of poverty. Even though the campaigners have denied these claims, most residents of the Yugan County have removed religious symbols indefinitely the moment this news broke out. This claim gained momentum a little after the C.P.C. conducted the national congress. In this national congress, General Secretary Xi managed to unify his party power and even drafted his political philosophy into the constitution of the congress. This single act had dramatically increased Xi's influence within the party. In fact, his power had grown to such an extent that the local newspaper even referred to him as *"the country's most powerful leader since Mao."*

In light of his popularity, Xi is adhering to the old tradition of Chinese leaders. This tradition is to forcefully implement state power and utilize it as a driving force to conquer opposing social movements. Way before the average Christian was forced to replace religious symbols with those of Xi, the Yugan church had already taken down its cross to seek peace with the government. This was a move followed by several churches in the Zhejiang area and other

Christian-dominated locations in recent years. Furthermore, by September 2017, the Chinese government had effectively initiated even tighter restrictions towards the Christian faith. These restrictions were implemented on an official basis in February 2018. However, before its implementation, a lot of provinces had to undergo severe crackdowns by governments. By December 2017, the government detained leaders of a house church and a three-year-old whose only crime was that he was singing in the public park.

Holistically, C.P.C.'s dominance over religion is typically exercised through the law. However, the party members are also carrying out their nefarious agendas through the integration of the religious doctrine with the party's communist views and practices. Although the concept of *"religion serving socialism"* has been present in the C.P.C. for quite some time, this abrasive and offensive intrusion of individual religions has become more widespread under the draconian dictatorship of Secretary Xi. Moreover, Xi, in one of his past speeches, instructed religious groups to *"dig deep into doctrines and canons that are in line with social harmony and progress... and interpret religious doctrines in a way that is conducive to modern China's progress and in line with our excellent traditional culture.*[14] Much like Xi, many local and national leaders of China are following similar policies and will not stop until Christianity and other religions are eliminated from the national culture. As of 2020, by using the guise of COVID-19, the government of China has developed and implemented several administrative measures to restrict the gatherings of religious groups. These policies were officially introduced on February 1, 2020, and they consisted of even harsher rules than 2018.

Although global attention is revolving around COVID-19, it appears that China is going on a completely different trajectory. Nowadays, this trajectory is referred to as the Sinicization of religion, and it is quickly becoming a trademark of China. As per the findings of Voice of Martyrs U.S.A., some of the requirements or criteria that Churches must adhere to include:

---

[14] Shellnutt (2017), China Tells Christians to replace images of Jesus with Communist President. Retrieved from https://www.christianitytoday.com/news/2017/november/china-christians-jesus-communist-president-xi-jinping-yugan.html

- Pastors need to present their sermons to the party official before delivering it.

- The Communist anthem should be sung at the commencement of any prayer.

- A Portrait of President Xi Jinping should be hung on the premises.

- Facial recognition cameras should be focused on the audience of the prayer or service.

The *Philosophy* of Sinicization

This philosophy is not a brand-new method of religious persecution. On the contrary, news agencies and media personnel believe that, *"Local officials have started to come into churches now and say, 'Wait a minute, you don't have a picture of President Xi in your sanctuary. What are you waiting for to put that up?' So, the pressure has just ratcheted up and up."* Normally, these underhanded actions were taken against the unregistered churches or house-based churches. However, in recent times, the government and its officials are even attacking churches that are registered in the town or local municipality. Judging from this, we can say that this is a well-thought-out plan to turn Christianity into another Chinese tradition. Only that form of Christianity doesn't contradict the party's ideology. In other words, this form of Christianity hails President Xi as a distinguished individual, even making him a god to be worshipped. For a staunch and ardent Bible-believing Christian, this is totally unacceptable, and it has resulted in various issues for the common man of faith.

Force, harassment, and the Communist Agenda

Christian persecution supervisory body China Aid highlights that, during the COVID-19 lockdown, the Chinese government had callously enforced its heinous policies against the country's churches. There have been more than three cases in which the Xi Administration forcibly removed the crosses in the lockdown. After assessing the stipulations, many religious experts and Christian authorities state that *"The Communist Party wishes to control the people. And they know for a fact that people who are sold out and committed to Jesus Christ are harder to control, so they don't want to allow the Gospel to spread. And if it does spread, they want it to be this sinicized version that honors the Communist Party and honors the Communist leaders. "*[15]

In the past, it was a common practice for the people of China to hang pictures of Communist leader Mao Zedong in the center of their homes. However, Xi Jinping has modified his image to resemble the illustrious headshot of Mao. This is a clear indication that President Xi Jinping is developing a personality cult, much like the founding father of the People's Republic of China.

Surprisingly enough, religion and its practice are not officially banned in the country. Yet still, the government and its various bodies force people not to fulfill their obligations. In spite of these fatalistic policies, Christianity has been spreading swiftly ever since the demise of Chairman Mao's Cultural Revolution.

The Cultural Revolution transpired more than four decades ago. Despite this, more and more people are coming to faith in the Lord Jesus Christ and many unsanctioned Churches have sprung up in people's homes. According to

---

[15] Klama (2020), China: The Sinicization of the Church. Retrieved from https://www.mnnonline.org/news/china-the-sinicization-of-the-church/

some estimates, the number of Christians has exceeded the total members of the Communist Party. According to the Freedom House report, close to one-third of believers, or roughly 100 million, are from religious groups that face constant persecution from Chinese authorities.

The report further added that several Christians are prevented from celebrating Christmas together. Moreover, ever since the commencement of 2014, local officials and government personnel have desperately tried to curb the spread of Christianity. They have done this through the propaganda of the threat of "Western" values and the necessity of *"Sinicizing religions."*

To justify their onslaught against innocent citizens, the Communist Party, specifically in Yugan, defends itself by revealing that the campaign was carried out *"willingly"* and was originally done to help the poor village-based community.[16] If we were to take the case of another prominent city of China, Chengdu, we would witness another heart-wrenching tale and tragedy. The situation in

---

[16] Maza (2017), Christians in China must replace Jesus with pictures of Xi Jinping or Lose Social Services. Retrieved from https://www.newsweek.com/china-christians-jesus-x-jinping-social-services-welfare-711090

Chengdu has worsened so much that in September 2017, Wang Yi, the pastor of one of China's famous underground churches, was forced to ask his congregation, *"If tomorrow morning the Early Rain Covenant Church suddenly disappeared from the city of Chengdu, if each of us vanished into thin air, would this city be any different? Would anyone miss us?"* After asking this depressing and very real question, Wang Yi, responded dismally, *"I don't know."*

Upon giving this sermon, Wang's supposed situation was tested out only three months later. This was because the Church in south-west China was closed, and Wang and his wife, Jiang Rong, were detained along with 100 Early Rain church members in December 2017. Those people who managed to escape detention somehow are still in hiding. All the while, several other believers have been exiled from Chengdu. The rest, which includes people like Wang's mother and his young son, are always kept under observation. Moreover, Wang and his wife will be charged for *"inciting subversion."* This misdemeanor results in a penalty of at least 15 years in prison.

In the present day, the grand hall where Wang used to deliver his sermons is empty. At the same time, the pulpit and cross that loomed in the Church are gone. Prayer cushions have been thrown away and replaced by a ping-pong table and a film of dust. New residents, a construction company, and a business association have filled the three floors of the Church. Moreover, police disguised in plainclothes stand guard and turn away any believer looking for the once enigmatic Church.

Sadly enough, Early Rain Church is only the latest fatality of what Chinese Christians and rights activists believe to be the worst crackdown on religion in history. Researchers highlight that this consolidated effort is not toward eliminating Christianity but taming it completely. This past year, local governments have shut down hundreds of unofficial *"house churches"* that function outside the government-approved church network, Churches like the unfortunate Early Rain. An official report, created and authorized by over 500 house church leaders in November 2019, stated that Chinese officials have replaced thousands of crosses from buildings, instructed churches to display the Chinese flag and sing patriotic songs, and even prohibited the entrance of minors. Many believers predict that the scenario may get far worse once it spreads over the entire country. Just recently, another home-based church in Chengdu was placed under surveillance. In addition to this, a few days following the mass arrest of Early Rain members, the Chinese police invaded a children's Sunday school in the city of Guangzhou. Furthermore, Chinese government officials have barred the 1,500-member Zion church in Beijing. They did this simply because the Church's pastor refused to comply with their demands to install an intrusive CCTV in the building.

In November 2019, the Guangzhou Bible Reformed Church was closed for the second time in only three months. Why did this occur? Well, the answer can be better described by the Church's pastor Huang Xiaoning. Huang Xiaoning, who recently stated that *"the Chinese Communist Party (C.C.P.) wants to be the god of China and the Chinese people. But according to the Bible, only God is God. The government is scared of the churches."* The paranoia of the Xi Jinping administration has become so high that local governments have even closed the state-approved "sanzi" churches. And, we can see the earliest signs of the crackdown when the Chinese establishment had effectively removed well over 1,000 crosses from sanzi churches in Zhejiang province between 2014 and 2016. According to Ying Fuk Tsang, the director of the Christian Study Centre on Chinese Religion and Culture at the Chinese University of Hong Kong, *"The primary objective of the crackdown is not to eradicate religions. On the other hand, President Xi Jinping is trying to establish a new order on religion, suppressing its blistering development. The Xi regime hopes to regulate the 'religious market' as a whole."*

The Chinese Communist Party (C.C.P.) may be atheist; however, Protestantism and Catholicism are two of five faiths officially sanctioned by the government. Since the 1980s, religious freedom is preserved in the Chinese constitution. For many decades, the Chinese government had accepted house churches and unofficial places of worship. In fact, the government had even tolerated those unofficial churches that had not registered with official bodies as it needed church leaders to comply and adhere to party doctrine. However, because China has recently witnessed an astonishing burst of religious believers, the government has become afraid of Christianity and Islam. Much like

Christians, the Muslim minorities, specifically the Uighurs, also had to endure surveillance and incarceration systems in Xinjiang. This clear violation of human rights occurred simply because General Secretary Xi wants the country to *protect* itself from *"penetration"* through religion and extremist ideology. Experts believe that the situation in Xinjiang and the persecution of house churches stem from the same principle.

In these perilous and turbulent times, courageous pastors, like Wang Yi of Early Rain, are a great threat for security and government officials. Because of Wang, who is also a legal scholar and intellectual, Early Rain had supported the parents of children killed in the 2008 Sichuan earthquake. These deaths, as per many critics, were caused by lackluster government-backed construction. Moreover, under the guidance of Wang, Early Rains and its officials had also compensated those families who had to suffer faulty vaccines. Furthermore, before the Church's ban and arrests, every year, Early Rain honored the victims of the June 4 protests of 1989. The Chinese military brutally eliminated these protests.

After Wang and his wife's detention, one of the members of the Church stated that *"Early Rain church is one of the few who dare to face what is wrong in society. Most churches don't dare talk about this, but we strictly obey the Bible, and we don't avoid anything."* Most new believers view Wang and Early Rain as a new generation of Christians, a generation that has surfaced along with a growing and much needed civil rights movement. In addition to Early Rain, activist church leaders are looking for change based on the democratizing role the Church played in several eastern European countries in the Soviet Union or South Korea under martial law. These activists also draw inspiration from the fact that a plethora of China's human rights lawyers are, in fact, Christians.

As of 2018, the Chinese government has implemented and issued several work plans to *ensure the nation's growth and prosperity.* Amongst these objectives, perhaps the most detrimental must be the government work plan for "promoting Chinese Christianity." This plan, which will span a period of four years, from 2018 to 2022, is referred to by General Secretary Xi Jinping as the *"thought reform."* The plan hopes to *"retranslate and interpret"* the Bible to discover commonalities with socialism and develop an *"accurate comprehension"* of the text. And, unfortunately, this plan is already underway. One of the first measures the Xi administration has taken is restricting the online purchases of the Holy Bible. Even though the Chinese government has always controlled Bible sales, in November 2019, the current administration has made the Holy Bible unavailable in the online marketplace. To make matters worse, just one month after this cruel action, Christmas festivities were banned in schools and cities across China.

Despite these challenges and overwhelming odds, the believers of the Christian faith continue to live on, and more and more people are gradually embracing the truth. Because of the belief in our Lord and Savior Jesus Christ, noble and fearless warriors like Wang Yi will continue to openly voice their opinions and say, *"In this war, in Xinjiang, in Shanghai, in Beijing, in Chengdu, the rulers have chosen an enemy that can never be imprisoned – the soul of man. Therefore, they are doomed to lose this war."*[17]

---

[17] Kuo (2019), In China, they're closing churches, jailing pastors-and even rewriting scripture. Retrieved from

This is the future we will look forward to once the plague of socialism and communism successfully engulfs our great nation. A future in which governments can freely violate basic human rights and get away with it without any consequences whatsoever. This is the future neoliberals and other socialist propagandists have in store for us, the people of the U.S.A., and the sooner we realize this fact, the better the chance we have of escaping this nightmare. As a result, I urge the youth of our great nation and my brothers and sisters in Christ to see the truth as it is and not be swayed by the smooth and misleading words of the dangerous cult of socialism and communism.

We, as a nation, need to educate ourselves about the evils of socialism and communism and make sure that our proud heritage of equality and freedom stands the will not become a thing of the past but will endure for generations to come. Armed with the knowledge in this book, Americans, especially the youth, will appreciate the blessings we enjoy in this nation, which guarantees our civil liberties, security, and economic wellbeing. It is my hope that this book has

---

https://www.theguardian.com/world/2019/jan/13/china-christians-religious-persecution-translation-bible#img-1

exposed socialism for what it truly is.

Appendix

Communism still thrives in Cuba largely

Communism in Venezuela.

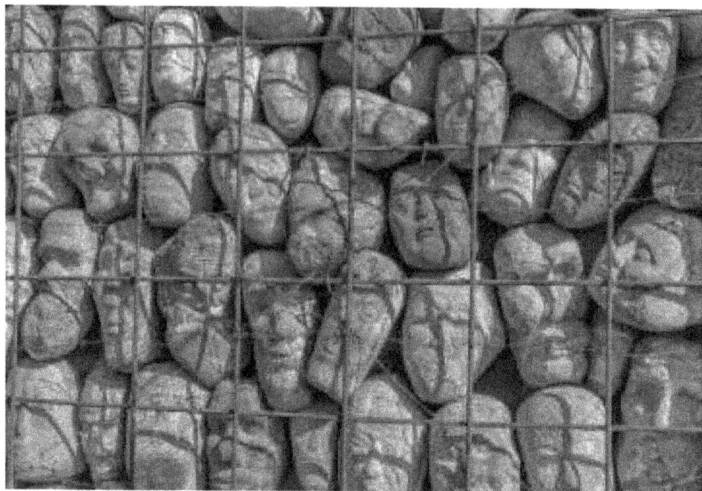

A Sculpture depicting the cruelty of the Soviet Communism in Gulag

A Soviet era mail stamp when Communism was at its peak.

Communism is running strong in China under the leadership of current President Xi Jinping.

Mao Zedong was the revolutionist that introduced Communism to this mighty country.

The sickle and the hammer have always been represented as symbols of Communism.

MOSES OLUWOLE, PH.D.